PROPHET
ON THE
RUN

A Devotional Commentary on the
Book of Jonah

BARUCH MAOZ

Shepherd Press
Wapwallopen, Pennsylvania

© 2013 by Baruch Maoz
Trade Paperback ISBN: 978-1936908-844

eBook ISBN
Kindle format: ISBN 978-1936908-899
ePub format: ISBN 978-1936908-882

Published by Shepherd Press
P.O. Box 24
Wapwallopen, Pennsylvania 18660

Page design and typesetting by Lakeside Design Plus
Cover design by Matthew Sample II

First Printing, 2013
Printed in the United States of America

VP 22 21 20 19 18 17 16 15 14 13
14 13 12 11 10 9 8 7 6 5 4 3 2 1

Library of Congress Control Number:
————————

Library of Congress Cataloging-in-Publication Data

Ma'oz, Barukh.
    Prophet on the run : devotional commentary on the Book of Jonah / Baruch Maoz.
        pages cm
    ISBN 978-1-936908-84-4 (print book : alk. paper)—ISBN 978-1-936908-89-9 (kindle ebook)—ISBN 978-1-936908-88-2 (epub ebook) 1. Bible.
Job—Commentaries. 2 Bible. Job—Devotional use. I. Title.
    BS1415.53.M36 2013
    224'.92077—dc23

                                                            2013040540

eBook Coupons
Free eBook for the purchaser of Prophet on the Run in Trade Paperback
Go to: http://www.shepherdpress.com/ebooks

Contents

Preface

The Bible is the word of God. Its message is relevant to men and women of every generation. But it is written in an ancient language (Hebrew, in Jonah's case) and with an assumed social and historical context that is generally unfamiliar to modern readers of the Bible.

Every language has its own poetry, its special way of conveying ideas. Every culture expresses its views of reality by different nuances. My goal in this book is to give the reader a graphic sense of the message of the book of Jonah, taking into account the particularities of Hebrew and of the historical background against which the narrative was written.

In an effort to achieve that goal, I have undertaken my own translation of the Hebrew so as to more clearly convey a sense of its poetry, its imagery and its flow so that the reader will be enabled to get at the author's intent without having to deal with technicalities. I sacrificed the English to serve the Hebrew. I hope readers will find reading my text helpful in spite of this, or rather, because of it.

This is not a study commentary. Others, better qualified, have provided excellent exegetical commentaries to the Bible. I would not presume to stand alongside them. Rather, I have learned much from them. This book is designed to convey an understanding of the biblical text, intimate some of its practical implications, and engage the reader in examining his heart and life in light of what he has learned. It is meant for Mr. and Mrs. Anybody, at just about any age.

Since its original publication in 2008, I have been gratified to learn that this little book has been beneficial to many around the globe, and that it has been used in personal devotions as well as by Bible study groups. I thank and praise God for his goodness.

I have preached series of sermons from the book of Jonah on a number of occasions, and been challenged afresh each time. This book is the product of those happy experiences. It is my prayer that my readers will be helped to love God and his word by reading this book, and that they will become eager, obedient students of God's word.

Gedera 2010

Introduction

For good reason, it is customary to begin a Bible commentary with an introduction which informs the reader about the book being studied, providing details about its author and his background, the book's historical context, its literary characteristics and other such information. Since this is not a technical commentary, this introduction is not required for understanding the book's message. Some readers will find it helpful, while others may wish to skip directly to the first chapter.

The Nature of the Book and the Date of Its Composition

Some Bible scholars believe that the book of Jonah is not a historical narrative but a literary fiction that was designed to convey a moral message. The primary motivation for such a view is an assumption: those who consider the book of Jonah to be fiction do not believe in miracles. We do, because we believe in God.

We do not assume miracles are commonplace. We recognize that God normally rules this world through the patterns he has established in nature and in the essence of all that exists. These are often spoken of as the Laws of Nature. These laws do not bind God; they merely describe the way he usually acts. A God who, with a mere word, called this amazing world into existence, who made everything out of nothing, would have no difficulty in arranging the chain of events described in the book of Jonah, including a large fish to swallow the prophet and spit him out onto dry ground three days later. It is possible that those who deny the existence of miracles do not, in fact, believe in God.

Scholars who deny the historical nature of the book of Jonah disagree about what kind of book it actually is. Some prefer to describe the book as an allegory; others insist it is a parable. Some say it is prose, while others claim it is a poem. Some state it is a *midrash* (a rabbinic story with a moral lesson); others read it as a symbolic narrative. We should not be unnerved by the claims and counter-claims of scholars. Scholarly views are as fluid as any other fashion, and they change as radically.

However, we can safely trust the unchanging Word of God. The Bible does not present the book of Jonah as anything but historical narrative. It is, of course, meant to convey a message, but that is true of all narratives. This story is meant to be considered as true as its message. That is probably why Jonah was placed among the prophets, not the poetic books.

The book of Jonah describes a series of events that occurred in the life of an historical figure who is referenced in another biblical text (2 Kings 14:25). There is no indication that the story is intended as an allegory or a parable.

Finally, our Lord Jesus referred to events narrated in this book in a manner that assumes their historical nature (Matt. 12:38–41, Luke 11:29–32, Matt. 16:4).

Some scholars date the writing of Jonah so late that the book is removed from its historical context and Jonah could have been neither its author nor the direct source of information for its composition. This view is largely based on the existence of a supposed Aramaic influence on the Hebrew text. Other scholars deny any such influence. Whether it exists or not, we need to remember that Jonah resided in the north of the country, not too far from Aram, and he lived during a time when Aram was at the peak of its power. This could easily explain an Aramaic influence on his language, should any be proven to exist.

Another argument for a late dating of the book's composition is based on quotations from what some scholars claim are post-exilic psalms—psalms that were written after Israel was deported to Babylon in the days of Hezekiah King of Judah and of Jeremiah the prophet.

This argument is unconvincing because there are just as many scholars who refuse to date those psalms so late—and who is to say if Jonah is quoting a psalm or a psalmist is quoting Jonah? It is more likely that Jonah was quoting the Psalms, but the opposite is also possible. In either case, such quotes cannot be used to determine a late date for the composition of the book of Jonah.

Nineveh was destroyed in 616 B.C. and the lack of any indication of that event in the book of Jonah firmly places the composition of the book before that time. During the years 782–745 B.C., the period in which we presume Jonah to have lived, Nineveh was under pressure from the northwestern kingdom of Urartu. This would have made the fulfillment of Jonah's prophecies all the more plausible to Nineveh's inhabitants. The facts of history seem to permit us to date the events narrated in the book of Jonah in the prophet's time, even if they do not conclusively prove when the book was written.

All this suggests that the book of Jonah was written sometime before the exile. In fact, since the content of Jonah's prayer could have only been disclosed by him, it seems likely that the book must have been written while the prophet was still alive, or at least by someone who had heard details from the prophet himself.

Jonah's narrative is unique among the prophetic books in that it is not a collection of prophetic utterances but a narrative—the story of what happened to a certain prophet at a certain time in his prophetic service.

The Language of the Book of Jonah

The author of this book had an impressive command of Hebrew. His language is rich, evocative and extremely well constructed. He avoids the emotional, incoherent and incomplete sentences with which Hosea addressed his nation. He uses none of the flowery terminology of Isaiah or the studied elegance of Habakkuk. In fact, the Hebrew is so well rounded that many Bible colleges and seminaries use the book of Jonah as part of their courses in biblical Hebrew.

The author was obviously a capable writer. He says no more than is necessary, uses vivid language, and describes events as building from one to the next. He displays a solid understanding of human nature, and employs a multitude of literary devices; humor, questions, ambivalent language, suggestive quotes and anthropomorphisms. Consequently, Jonah is a fun book to read and a fun book to study.

The book ends with a stunning question that calls upon the reader and the careful student of this book in every generation to respond. It is a masterpiece of spiritual and moral instruction. May we learn its lessons and make them part of our lives.

The Prophet

We learn from 2 Kings 14:25 that Jonah, the son of Amitai, prophesied in the northern kingdom of Israel in the early days of Jeroboam the Second (793–753 B.C.) or just before his reign—a peak of economic and military success in Israel's history.

Jonah lived in Gat Hefer in Galilee, in the portion of the land given to the tribe of Zebulon, between Nazareth and Cana. Gat Hefer has been excavated only to a limited extent although it is one of the largest mounds in Galilee. The excavations show that Gat Hefer was a large city, but the shortage of significant findings resulted in a lack of interest on the part of archeologists.

No reference is made elsewhere in the Old Testament to Jonah's call, attempted escape and journey to Nineveh, or to any of the other events described in the book of Jonah.

Nothing more is known of the prophet, his message to Israel, his family, his life or his death. Seven locations lay claim to be the place of his burial—anywhere from south-central Israel to the ancient site of Nineveh in what is northern Iraq today.

Purpose of the Book

The book of Jonah is extraordinary in that Jonah is the only prophet of Israel actually sent to another nation. Amos, Isaiah,

Jeremiah, Ezekiel and Habakkuk all prophesied about other nations, but what they said was addressed to Israel and meant for Israel's comfort and encouragement. Jonah's message was delivered in a foreign country, to a foreign people. Whatever lessons the people of Israel (or Judah) were to receive from the prophet's life and message, they were to learn indirectly.

The central message of the book is much needed and highly relevant to Jewish ears: Israel has no ownership over God. He is the God of all nations. All owe him obedience, and he shows mercy to all without distinction. This message anticipates the message of the New Testament—that God has taken Jews and Gentiles, set aside the differences between them, and made of the two one new people in Christ.

It is also a relevant message for our day and for the church. In this age of extreme individualism, our differences—national, cultural and linguistic—have been permitted to divide the church. This should not be.

Other important lessons that may be learned from the book of Jonah have to do with the kindness and sovereignty of God, the impossibility of resisting him, his rule over nature and all nations, the need to accept responsibility for our deeds, God's amazing patience, and the nature of true repentance.

Outline of the Book of Jonah

The four chapters of the English Bible more or less correspond with a natural division of the book. There is one difference compared to the Hebrew: the last verse in chapter 1 in the English Bible is the first of chapter 2 in Hebrew. But we need not quibble over such a matter. Following the English Bible, the outline of the book would be as follows:

Chapter 1—Jonah Tries to Escape

Chapter 2—The Prophet Asleep and Ensnared

Chapter 3—Jonah Takes Responsibility for His Actions

Chapter 4—The Prophet Repents

1

Jonah Tries to Escape

1:1–4

✳

The word of the Lord came to Jonah the son of Amitai: "Get up, go to Nineveh, that great city, and call out against her because their evil has come up before me." And Jonah got up, to flee to Tarshish from the presence of the Lord. He went down to Joppa, found a ship going to Tarshish, paid the fare, and went on board to flee from the presence of the Lord.

But the Lord hurled a great wind onto the sea, and there was a great storm on the sea, and the ship considered breaking up. (vv. 5-16) The sailors feared and cried out, each to his own god, and they cast the containers into the sea to make (the ship) lighter for them—and Jonah had descended into the ship's hold, lain down, and slept.

The captain drew near to him and said, "What's wrong with you, sleeper! Get up, call to your god, it may be that god will think of us and we will not perish!"

And they said one to another, "Let's cast lots and discover on whose account this evil has happened to us." And they cast lots, and the lot fell on Jonah. They said to him, "Tell us, you, because of whom evil has happened to us, what is your occupation and where do you come from, which is your country and to which nation do you belong?"

And he said to them, "I am a Hebrew, and it is the God of heaven that I fear, who made the sea and the dry land." And the people feared a great fear and said to him, "What is this that you have done!" because the people knew that he was fleeing from the presence of the Lord, because he had told them. So they said to him, "What shall we do to you, so that the seas will stop shrieking above us?" (Because the sea was becoming increasingly stormier).

And he said to them, "Lift me up and throw me into the sea and the sea will stop shrieking over you, because I know that because of me this great storm is upon you." But the people rowed to return to the dry land, but could not because the sea was increasingly stormier against them.

So they cried out to the Lord and said, "Please, Lord, let us not perish because of the death of this man and do not hold us accountable for the death of an innocent, because you, O Lord, have done what you wished." And they lifted Jonah and threw him into the sea, and the sea's anger was relaxed. And the people greatly feared the Lord, so they offered the Lord a sacrifice and made vows to him.

✳

> The word of the Lord came to Jonah the son of Amitai: "Get up, go to Nineveh, that great city, and call out against her because their evil has come up before me." And Jonah got up, to flee from the presence of the Lord.

The Call—Verse 1

Like so many stories in the Bible, Jonah's story begins with God. God turns to Jonah the son of Amitai with a clear, unequivocal command: "Get up, go to Nineveh, that great city, and call out against her because their evil has come up before me."

Nineveh was a major city in the Neo-Assyrian Empire. In the previous century, Assyria had been a major military power, conquering the Arameans and forcing the Israelites to pay tribute. But in the days of Jereboam's reign and Jonah's ministry (793–753 B.C.), Assyria experienced an economic, political, and military recession that would end only in 745 B.C. following the ascension of Tiglath-Pileser III to the throne. Consequently, Assyria did not pose a serious threat to Israel during Jonah's lifetime.

In spite of Assyria's relative weakness, it remained rich, ambitious and confident. Riches brought corruption. The Assyrians practiced idolatry, and Nineveh had for centuries been a center of pagan worship. Their idolatrous practices encouraged a shortsighted hedonism that undermined the roots of the nation's power. They sought immediate gain rather than morality which would create social cohesion and lasting strength, as Proverbs 14:34 teaches: "Righteousness exalts a nation, but sin is a disgrace to any people."

This is the environment into which God sent Jonah. He instructed Jonah to "call out against her"—to declare in Nineveh that God is about to bring punishment on the city, because the Ninevites led lives that were evil in God's sight. Because God is not only the God of Israel, but the Lord over all the nations of the world, even those who are not in covenant with him are not free to live their lives as they wish. They are still bound by his will and must live according to the moral standards that he has established.

It is wrong to think that non-Christians are free from God's law. All people are bound by God's law, and all will be judged by it. Paul tells us that God's anger "is being revealed from heaven against all the godlessness and wickedness of men" (Rom. 1:18), be they Jewish or Gentile, believers or unbelievers. "All who sin apart from the law will also perish apart from the law, and all who sin under the law will be judged by the law" (Rom. 2:12).

"Because their evil has come up before me"—this is the foundation for gospel preaching. Only when we recognize our sin in contrast with God's holiness will we understand our need of a savior from the consequences of wrongdoing.

This idea creates a real measure of discomfort. But it is also very comforting because it teaches us that all of our deeds are important because they have moral implications. Our deeds count in God's sight. Obviously, it is not a good thing if our deeds are evil in his sight, but at least they have value! If what we do matters to God, how much more must we matter to him? This simple fact lays the ground for hope, because if God is interested in us, perhaps he will also be kind toward us.

In spite of this, many people live as if there is no point in praying or turning to God at all—they assume that he is busy with more important things, if he even exists. This is not what we learn from Jonah. *Their evil has come up before me* means that he takes note of them. What they do really does matter to God.

The book of Jonah teaches us that God holds people accountable for their deeds. He punishes those who act wickedly, because he is *the* righteous *Judge of all the earth*. As we shall see, he is also the God of mercy and of grace, rewarding those who repent. But God's grace does not remove his utter hatred for sin, nor does it erase his determination to punish anyone who persists in sin and refuses to turn to him. "God will give to each person according to what he has done. To those who by persistence in doing good seek glory, honor and immortality, he will give eternal life. But for those who are self-seeking and who reject the truth and follow evil, there will be wrath and anger" (Rom. 2:6–8).

After conversion, recognition of sin and God's holiness is also foundational for healthy Christian living. It teaches us humility and drives us to trust in God rather than in our own achievements. It drives us to seek forgiveness from and reconciliation with people we have sinned against. Christ indeed atoned for our sin by bearing its guilt and punishment, but sinful deeds are still violations of God's law, and Christ's atoning work does not erase such deeds from the annals of history any more than it undoes many of their consequences. Whoever stole must, upon conversion, return the stolen goods. Whoever divorced his or her spouse on unbiblical grounds must do everything morally possible to be reconciled.

The Prophet's Response—Verses 2–3

So the command came, "Get up, go to Nineveh, that great city, and call out against her because their evil has come up before me."

The author begins his description of the prophet's response just as anyone in his right mind would expect: God commanded him, "Get up," and Jonah got up. The next phrase, we assume, will be "and went to Nineveh." After all, Jonah was a prophet of God. Earlier (in 2 Kings 14:25), he had prophesied the growth of Jeroboam's kingdom, and it came about exactly as he had predicted. Wouldn't a prophet naturally—even enthusiastically—do exactly what God commanded?

Not this prophet. *Jonah got up—to flee to Tarshish from the presence of the Lord.* What madness! What a senseless thing for a prophet to do! Why would a prophet of God think he could escape from God's presence? How could a prophet believe that he could ignore God's command?

We learn here that men of God are not free of faults, sin or weakness. Jonah followed in a long line of people who served God but fell into sin. Abraham handed his wife over—twice!—to save his own neck. Jacob lied, taking advantage of his brother's weak character and his father's blindness. David sinned with Bathsheba. Jonah defied God's direct command and fled from the presence of the Lord.

If we are honest, we must admit that we are no different. None of God's people are without sin. We will never be completely free of sin until the day when we shall be freed by the power of God's grace and the work of the Holy Spirit, at the revelation of God's eternal kingdom.

The story of Jonah should encourage us to pray for those who serve us in the gospel. Like Jonah, although they are called to do God's work, they too stumble and fall—like us, they are not perfect. Because they are subject to greater pressures and temptations than those that face most of us, their struggle with sin is all the more difficult.

We should not expect them to be perfect. We should learn to support them in their weakness by giving them our forgiveness, support and comfort. We should encourage them in their struggles and help them improve their spiritual lives. We should seek ways to support their efforts to develop their walk with Christ, and we should pray for them.

We should give them a real measure of privacy, send them to helpful courses and seminars that will cultivate their spiritual walk, make sure they take vacations, and enable them to purchase good, helpful literature. We should love them because God loves us through them. If we love them as we should, we will be loving and serving ourselves.

We also learn that sin stupefies those who fall into its claws. Note the author's words: *Jonah got up to flee . . . from the presence of the Lord.* But where could he flee? Surely he was familiar with the words David had written years before, Where can I go from your Spirit?

> Where can I flee from your presence? If I go up to the heavens, you are there; if I make my bed in the depths, you are there. If I rise on the wings of the dawn, if I settle on the far side of the sea, even there your hand will guide me, your right hand will hold me fast. If I say, "Surely the darkness will hide me and the light become night around me," even the darkness will not be dark to you, the night will shine like the day, for darkness is as light to you (Ps. 139: 7–12).

Jonah's act recalls Adam and Eve's ridiculous effort to hide in the Garden of Eden after they had sinned, vainly concealing themselves among the trees of the garden so that the God who sees everything would not see them and the God who knows everything would not know where they were. Jonah later confessed that God made the sea and the dry land (v. 9). If he knew that to be true, what was the point of his trying to flee from the Lord, even if he took a ship all the way to Tarshish?

There was no point. When we give in to sin, sin takes over our thought processes and causes us to act foolishly, against all logic and contrary to everything we know. Sin makes us stupid.

Attempting the Impossible

The author's language is sharp and colorful. He depicts a series of rapidly executed actions, one after the next, and he groups them all in one sentence to give us a sense of immediacy: "He went down to Joppa, found a ship going to Tarshish, paid the fare, and went on board to flee from the presence of the Lord."

Jonah came from Gat Hefer in Galilee. It would have been natural for him to have fled north, to nearby Tyre or Sidon. Many ships berthed at these ports and they could have taken him just about anywhere. But Jonah decided to run in the exact opposite direction—as if he could outwit God by such a diversion.

Tarshish was probably a port city near present-day Barcelona, Spain—at the far end of the known world. A voyage from Joppa to Tarshish took approximately one year, and Jonah thought that if he could distance himself so far from the land of Israel, he might also be able to distance himself from Israel's God. The writer emphasizes this by twice repeating the words *from the presence of the Lord* in the space of two sentences.

Jonah's problem was not with what he knew, because he clearly had substantial theological knowledge. He already knew what he needed to know. He certainly knew that the Lord rules over all. The problem was that his theology had not sufficiently penetrated his heart and his way of life. He acted against what he knew.

That is not the way to use Christian knowledge. What we know should direct our actions. Christ said, "If you know these things, happy are you if you do them" (John 13:17 ESV).

God's Response—Verse 4

Jonah sought to flee from the presence of the Lord, but the Lord had other plans for him. After Jonah's five energetic actions–he arose, went down to Joppa, found a ship, paid the fare and went down into its hold–God responded with a single action: *the Lord hurled a great wind onto the sea.*

The language is dramatic, suggestive and terse. God did not simply "send" a strong wind onto the sea. He did not merely "command" the wind to blow mightily on the sea. He actively *hurled a great wind onto the sea*, as a man who lifts a great stone and casts it down. Something of Jehovah's anger is revealed here, something of his terrible strength.

Jonah's God is the God of all the powers of nature. When he wishes, the wind blows and the sea becomes stormy. Nature does not act on its own; Jehovah is actively involved in all its processes, and when Jonah tried to flee from his presence, he *hurled a great wind onto the sea*. In consequence, *the ship considered breaking up.*

Once again, the language is evocative. The author speaks of the ship as if it were a person struggling with the storm—moaning and groaning, breathing heavily, and finally giving up rather than continuing to fight against the wind and the waves. The powers of nature and even the ship itself all cooperate with God in putting an end to the prophet's vain effort to escape from the presence of the Lord.

Summary

1. Jehovah is the God of all nations. He has entered into covenantal relationship with Israel, but he is not indifferent

to other nations. They are all important to him and will all be judged by him. His saving grace is not limited to the people of Israel; the borders of his grace encompass all that exist. God has a real interest in what people do. Our lives have value beyond what we eat or drink, how much we can enjoy life or multiply. God attributes moral value to our actions. What we do matters to God.

2. Sin leads to punishment. The people of Nineveh were living sinfully and God was preparing to punish them in response. But, in God's world, grace often preempts punishment, and God sent Jonah to warn the Ninevites of his anger and impending punishment.

3. All humans are duty-bound to satisfy the righteousness of God as presented in the Law. All will be judged by the Law. The right way to preach the gospel of Christ is to begin with this foundational truth. Only when people understand God's holiness and see their sin in light of that holiness will they also understand their need of a savior.

4. Jehovah is the God of all humankind—of those who believe in him and serve him and of those who do not. Our actions prior to conversion are not annulled by our conversion. Jesus saves us from the guilt and penalty of those sins, but many of their consequences remain. It is our duty to do everything within our power to put right what we have done wrong.

5. Like Jonah, the servants of the Lord are not perfect. Like Jonah, they also sin. We should pray for those who serve us in the gospel, support them in love, forgive them when they fail, and encourage them to improve and continue to serve both God and us.

6. Sin makes us stupid. Sometimes it masquerades as wisdom, but the "wisdom" of sin is artificial. It is worldly and it

blinds us to the truth. In the long run, it will be exposed as shortsighted foolishness.

7. It is better to be wary of sin and not to be attracted to its false promises. Jonah knew better, but he acted as if it were possible to escape the presence of the Lord. He acted contrary to what he knew, as we all do when we sin. We should be on our guard against sin by constantly reminding ourselves of the truths of God's Word and by carefully living according to them.

8. God rules over all, including the powers of nature. He can cause storms, and he can silence them; give life and take it away. We should trust him, love him, and persist in faithful service to him. We should rejoice in his abilities and always turn to him for everything in every situation—because there is no situation over which he does not have control.

Prayer

Lord, teach us to trust you and,
when we have trusted,
to lovingly obey.
In the name of your Son, Jesus,
Amen.

Questions for Discussion

1. What have you learned about Nineveh?

2. What have you learned about man and his relationship to God? Note in particular issues of covenant and of law.

3. List all that was contrary to logic and all that was sinful in Jonah's attempt to escape. What is the relationship between the two? What does this teach you about the nature of sin?

4. What have you learned about God?

5. How does God respond to sin?

2

The Prophet Asleep
and Ensnared

1:5–6

*

*The word of the Lord came to Jonah the son of Amitai:
"Get up, go to Nineveh, that great city, and call out
against her because their evil has come up before me."
And Jonah got up, to flee from the presence of the Lord.*

—*Jonah 1:1-3*

As we saw, Jonah fled after God commanded him to warn the people of Nineveh about God's impending judgment. Jonah went to Joppa, found a ship preparing to embark on a long journey, paid the fare, and boarded the ship. With others, he began his journey toward Tarshish, located in the far western corner of the Mediterranean Sea. In spite of what he knew to be true, he believed that he could escape from his God-given duty.

But God had other plans. He cast a mighty wind onto the sea, causing such a violent storm that the ship's crew—all experienced sailors, accustomed to storm-ridden voyages—panicked. Voyages to Tarshish were lengthy and dangerous. Only the most skilled, competent sailors were normally employed for such a voyage. They had seen storms in their lifetime, but they had never seen a storm like this!

The Sleepy Prophet—Verse 5

> The sailors feared and cried out, each to his own god, and they cast the containers into the sea to make (the ship) lighter for them—and Jonah had descended into the ship's hold, lain down, and slept. The captain drew near to him and said, "What's wrong with you, sleeper! Get up, call to your god, it may be that god will think of us and we will not perish!"

Try to imagine: the wind howled, the waves crashed against the ship and washed over the deck. The raging sea tossed the ship about as if it were a discarded nutshell as the ship's masts groaned against the wind. The sailors shouted warnings and instructions to each other, here struggling to tie down a sail, there frantically throwing a loose barrel overboard. Fear gripped the sailors' hearts until they despaired.

The sailors feared and cried out, each to his own god, and they cast the containers into the sea to make (the ship) lighter for them.

One good thing can be said of these sailors: they prayed. If this was not a time to pray, what would be? Fear drove them to cry out to their gods for help. Yet the "gods" of the nations are none-gods. They cannot help. The sailors were trusting in nothingness, in idols that cannot even move a hand or bat an eyelid.

Do you pray in times of trial? Do you turn to your god? Do you have a god to whom you can turn? Or do you, like Jonah, go down into the hold and try to escape reality through sleep or other means? If so, the words that the sailors spoke to Jonah apply to you as well: *"What's wrong with you, sleeper! Get up, call to your god!"*

God loves our company. Why? I do not know. But from what is said in Scripture I learn that God wants us to turn to him, seek his face and rejoice in his company. Sometimes, as with Jonah, God even brings storms into our lives to stir us to prayer. It really is a shame that we pray so rarely!

When the sailors saw that their prayers were not being answered, they began to take the customary and necessary measures in such circumstances: "They cast the containers into the sea to make (the ship) lighter for them."

Such a measure was taken only when there was no other way to save the ship, because in those days ships were primarily built for the transport of goods. There were no dedicated passenger ships; travelers booked passage on whichever ship was bound for their intended destination. The ship's cargo was the very reason for the voyage. It represented the significant material resources of the ship and of all who hired it for the voyage. The labor of years and the livelihood of all involved were invested in the cargo. But a situation had arisen in which all this was no longer important. The only thing that mattered was saving the ship, its passengers and the crew. The cargo had to be jettisoned.

Cargo would be thrown overboard when the ship had begun to fill with water and become so heavy that it was in danger of sinking. Lightening the load could cause the ship to roll more forcefully and even capsize. Only the weight of the water flowing into the ship would keep it from doing so—and that weight might itself sink the ship with all its passengers. What a dilemma! Yet there was nothing else the sailors could do.

While all this was happening, we are told that Jonah had descended into the ship's hold, lain down, and slept. This is hard to believe, really hard. How could he sleep in such a situation, with the ship tossing on the sea and the sailors shouting frantically above deck? He must have been drenched as well—because of the way ships were built in those days, there is no doubt that Jonah's bed was almost as wet as the deck.

It seems that the prophet's deep sleep was but another aspect of his effort to escape the presence of the Lord. When we don't want to cope with life, we tend to pull down the shutters, turn off the light, cover our heads with a blanket, and try to sleep until our problems go away. Like children, we tend to think that if we cannot see we cannot be seen; if we just sleep, all the trials of life will disappear.

The trouble is that our trials will wait for us at our bedside and be the first to greet us when we awake. We will still have to deal with them. Christians have no reason to try to escape life, because they rule in life through Jesus the Messiah (Rom. 5:17). The grace of God supports them and the love of God accompanies them in all their ways. We must not go down into the ship's hold and sleep. We need to get up and call upon our God.

The Need to Pray—Verse 6

"The captain drew near to him and said, 'What's wrong with you, sleeper! Get up, call to your god, it may be that god will think of us and we will not perish!'" Sometimes we need an idolatrous pagan, like the captain of the ship in which Jonah traveled, to remind us of the right thing to do.

"It may be," the captain said. At least at that moment the captain knew what everyone who fears God knows very well—that prayers can't force God to do anything; rather, everything depends on the sovereign, divine will of the creator of this world, not on the power of our prayers.

The kind of doubt that the captain expressed is not a lack of faith. It is a good and proper recognition of God's freedom to act as he sees fit and his right to do with man whatever he wills. We should never think that we can pray in such a way as to force God to grant our requests. We should not try to exchange roles with him. He governs both the world and our fates. Willingly or otherwise, we are his servants. His will is to be done, not ours, and that is the way things should be.

We are not told that Jonah prayed—why would he pray when he knows full well that the terrible storm was a result of his disobedience? How could he turn to God and seek his blessing when he was fleeing God's presence and refusing to do God's will? Like Jonah, we cannot expect the blessing of God when we sin, nor are we entitled to seek it. Apparently, Jonah did not pray. His conscience silenced him and kept him from doing so.

Do you find it difficult to pray? Could it be that the reason is that you are trying to escape God, that you are being disobedient to him? We should examine our hearts, and we should be encouraged to do so by the knowledge that God is the God of mercy and of grace, the God of salvation and of forgiveness, a God who loves to forgive sinners.

The story of Jonah illustrates this clearly, as we will see later. It is shown even more clearly in the life, death, and resurrection of Jesus Christ. In the sacrifice of God's Son, God did not send his Son into the world to punish the world for its sins, as we might have expected. Rather, he sent him to atone for sins. He now invites us all to come to him and find in him comfort, forgiveness and a renewed hope for life.

This is one of the world's greatest wonders: that the God of heaven and earth, the creator and sustainer of all that exists, he who needs nothing at all, who exists by virtue of his eternal, glorious Godhood, takes an interest in human beings and pays attention to their prayers.

As we shall see, this is how Jonah thought of God's grace and, finally, it was on that grace that he leaned.

The Prophet Discovered—Verses 7–9

And they said one to another, "Let's cast lots and discover on whose account this evil has happened to us." And they cast lots, and the lot fell on Jonah. They said to him, "Tell us, you, because of whom evil has happened to us, what is your occupation and where do you come from, which is your country and to which nation do you belong?"

And he said to them, "I am a Hebrew, and it is the God of heaven that I fear, who made the sea and the dry land." And the people feared a great fear and said to him, "What is this that you have done!" because the people knew that he was fleeing from the presence of the Lord, because he had told them.

Prayer brought no help—and why should it have? The "gods" that the sailors prayed to were no gods at all, and they were unable to do anything. Idols are worthless. People who worship them are blind and ignorant, and will be put to shame (see Isaiah 44:9–17).

How can anyone expect an idol to control a storm? Only the true God, whose will governs everything, can do this, and he alone can answer prayer. Unlike the idolatrous sailors, we have ample reason to pray. We can pray confidently because God's heart is soft toward us in Christ, and through Christ he extends his love to us.

When their prayers went unanswered, the sailors turned one to another and said, "Let's cast lots and discover on whose account this evil has happened to us." They believed that some kind of moral or spiritual wisdom governed the affairs of the world, and if all their efforts to overcome the storm failed, the cause of the storm was likely to be found among the ship's passengers. It was clear to the crew that *this evil* had come upon them because of someone on the vessel, and they decided to find out who he was.

They also believed that a divine power governed all things and, therefore, that casting lots would identify the person who had brought evil upon them (see Prov. 16:33). They did not understand, however, that divine control over all things does not eliminate man's duty to investigate, inquire, weigh the evidence, and arrive at conclusions. That is why they did not employ the proper means to discover who had brought this difficulty upon them. Instead, they chose to cast lots, *and the lot fell on Jonah.*

God in his grace uses even inappropriate methods, such as the lots employed by these unbelievers. After the lot fell on Jonah, the sailors turn to him and ask, "Tell us, you, because of whom evil has happened to us, what is your occupation and where do you come from, which is your country and to which nation do you belong?"

Their question was sharp and accusing, and carried an implied threat. Jonah bore responsibility for the raging storm that threatened to kill them all. The sailors and passengers did not absolve him of his guilt. One might have expected them to try to persuade him with gentle, flattering words, in the hope that he would cooperate. But his guilt was clear and he had to accept it.

It is right to act mercifully and kindly toward those who do wrong, but we must never deny their responsibility for their actions. It is often right to forgive and to relieve a sinner of the sense of guilt that he bears, but we must not rob him of responsibility for his actions, nor deny his duty to turn to God and find cleansing, forgiveness and restoration.

The sailors asked about Jonah's occupation and origin— which country and which people he had come from. In this way they confronted the prophet with his sin. There was no escaping his responsibility for his sinful behavior. He was forced to own up to his sins–he could no longer deny them.

Accountability—Verse 10

Accepting responsibility for sin is an essential aspect of forsaking sin. So long as we continue to make excuses, minimize the seriousness of our offenses and ignore our responsibility, we cannot be saved. We should not hedge our apologies with all kinds of excuses and conditional statements (such as "If I offended you . . ."). We should be mature and accept responsibility for our actions. Then the forgiveness can also be full. The Scripture says, "He who conceals his sins does not prosper, but whoever confesses and renounces them finds mercy" (Prov. 28:13).

Note the two parts of the verse we have just quoted. The first part warns against trying to hide our sins, and the second provides us with an excellent reason to acknowledge them. *Whoever confesses and renounces (his sins) finds mercy.*

Sadly, we do not always extend mercy to those who confess. We sometimes like to celebrate on the graves of our friends and to dance on the beaten bodies of those who led us in the past.

God is different. He is holy and merciful, quick to forgive because he loves forgiving. He is slow to anger, so much so that the Bible describes anger as something that is "strange" to him (Isa. 28:21). He promises mercy to all who confess and renounce their sins. As we continue in our study we shall see that this was the principle that motivated the sailors, who chose at first not to cast Jonah into the sea but did everything they could to save him.

Jonah answered the sailors' questions, but the writer does not provide the prophet's complete answer. From verse 11 we learn that Jonah said more than is quoted. The writer focuses on one main thing: Jonah said, "I am a Hebrew, and it is the God of heaven that I fear, who made the sea and the dry land."

Jonah's words created a tremendous sense of foreboding in the sailors' hearts. They believed that there were a multitude of gods, one for every part of the world and aspect of life: the god of Assyria and the god of Israel, the god of Egypt and the god of Sidon, the god of fertility and the god of storms, the god of the seas and the god of dry land. Jonah, on the other hand, spoke of one god, the God of heaven who created the dry land as well as the seas.

From Jonah's description, the sailors knew that this was a God with unlimited rule and who had power over everything, because "the Maker is also the Master of his creation."[1] Jonah's God rules over all three spheres of creation, including the sea and the terrifying storm that tossed their ship about. It was therefore natural that *the people feared a great fear.* They obviously understood that if Jehovah was the true God, then he was very angry, and they were in serious trouble.

---

[1] Uriel Simon, *A Scientific Commentary to the Scripture, Obadiah-Jonah,* Am Oved Publishing House Ltd., Tel Aviv, Magnes Press, the Hebrew University, Jerusalem, 1992.

The sailors addressed Jonah with a clear rebuke: "'What is this that you have done!' because the people knew that he was fleeing from the presence of the Lord, because he had told them." From the explanation that follows the rebuke, we learn that the sailors' words were not intended to express an inquiry but to charge the prophet with guilt. From what follows we learn that Jonah had already told them what he had done.

The charge is not "what have you done to us!" but *what is this that you have done*, directing Jonah's attention (and ours) to the deed rather than to its consequences. Their question forces Jonah to think about his actions and to see them in a new light. He had rebelled against God! On top of that, he had involved others in his rebellion and brought on them the consequences of his sin. How could he be so indifferent to the fate of others, to the extent that he would be willing to endanger them?

It is important to understand that our sins always have consequences, and that these consequences are sometimes far-reaching. Our sins affect others whose lives intersect with ours. Jonah's sin endangered the ship's sailors and passengers, even though none of them shared in his guilt.

Parents, beware! Your sins can have damaging consequences for your children. They may share in the punishment that falls on you for your sins. We should thank God for this warning and use it well by avoiding any act that will adversely affect our loved ones and those committed to our care.

Other examples of this are found throughout Scripture: Achan's sin led to catastrophic military defeat; David's sin resulted in an epidemic that affected thousands of his people; the writer of the letter to the Hebrews warns his readers not to permit a root of bitterness to spring up in the church and defile many; and Adam's sin corrupted the whole human race.

How we choose to live affects our children and those who surround us, far and near. No man is an island and no man is a world to himself. That is exactly why we must watch over each other, encourage each other to do well and stir each other to act in a worthy manner. We need each other as we walk the way of God.

Summary

1. Man plans his ways, but God determines the consequences of what man does, and God fulfills all his purposes, often in spite of man.

2. We need to pray often. We need to persist in prayer. God by his grace loves our company.

3. We should never think we can obligate God by our prayers. He is the Sovereign, not we. *It may be that god will think of us and we will not perish*. Such doubt is not an expression of unbelief, but of our acceptance of God's right to act as he pleases.

4. There are many good reasons to pray. Not only does God command us to pray, but his grace calls us to turn to him.

5. It is impossible to escape from God. He is everywhere and rules over all. The very sea on which Jonah sought to escape from God cooperated with God to prevent his flight.

6. Sin creates a distance between God and us, making it difficult to pray. This in itself is a good reason not to sin.

7. Our sins have far-reaching consequences. They affect others far beyond anything we might imagine, just as Adam's sin affected all of humankind. So we need to be on our guard to avoid sinning.

8. We cannot escape the consequences of our actions. Trying to do so is tantamount to escaping salvation. Recognition of our sin and an acceptance of our guilt, however painful, is the first necessary step toward salvation. So we should not try to avoid responsibility, but face it bravely. We will then find that salvation awaits us.

Prayer

Lord God,
who made the sea, the dry land and all that is in them,
work in our hearts so that we will obey you
and never try to escape you.
Teach us to be sensitive to those who surround us
and not fall asleep like Jonah did,
but to pray much, often, persistently.
Have mercy on us for the sake of your Son, Jesus, Amen.

Questions for Discussion

1. How do we act when influenced by sin?

2. What does sin do to our prayer life? How does it affect us and how does it affect others?

3. What have you learned about prayer?

4. What have you learned about God?

5. What is accountability and why is it important?

3

Jonah Takes Responsibility for His Actions

1:9–16

And he said to them, "I am a Hebrew, and it is the God of heaven that I fear, who made the sea and the dry land." And the people feared a great fear and said to him, "What is this that you have done!" because the people knew that he was fleeing from the presence of the Lord, because he had told them. So they said to him, "What shall we do to you, so that the seas will stop shrieking over us?" (Because the sea was becoming increasingly stormier).

And he said to them, "Lift me up and throw me into the sea and the sea will stop shrieking over you, because I know that because of me this great storm is upon you." But the people rowed to return to the dry land, but could not because the sea was increasingly stormier against them.

So they cried out to the Lord and said, "Please, Lord, let us not perish because of the death of this man and do not hold us accountable for the death of an innocent, because you, O Lord, have done what you wished." And they lifted Jonah and threw him into the sea, and the sea's anger was relaxed. And the peo-

*ple greatly feared the Lord, so they offered the Lord a sacrifice
and made vows to him.*

Handling Guilt—Verses 11–12

Jonah was asked, "Tell us, you, because of whom evil has happened to us, what is your occupation and where do you come from, which is your country and to which nation do you belong?" The sailors and passengers described Jonah as the one because of whom the storm had occurred and was now threatening them. Their words convey a direct rebuke: *you, because of whom evil has happened to us.*

Jonah knew he was guilty. Later on he will say, *I know that because of me this great storm is upon you.* But for as long as he thought that he could evade responsibility, he remained silent. The storm did not stir his conscience; nor did the danger he had brought on his fellow passengers, or the damage he caused them when they were forced to throw the ship's cargo into the sea.

Jonah was completely occupied with his efforts to flee the presence of God at any cost, and he knew that acknowledgement of his responsibility would amount to facing God himself. That is exactly what he did not want to do. So he kept his silence. Like many of us, he acted in violation of everything he knew and believed—but now his guilt was clear for all to see.

Jonah ignored their rebuke. He chose not to hear it. He had not responded to the captain's previous admonition and did not turn to prayer. Now, instead of heeding this reproof and responding to it, he carried on as if nothing happened. Finally the passengers turned to him again and asked, "What shall we do to you, so that the seas will stop shrieking over us?"

Their question was not, "What shall we do," or even "What will you do?" but "What shall we do to you?" It had become clear to them that they had to do something, and that that something must be done to Jonah, because he had brought the storm upon them.

We love the freedom to act and the right to decide for ourselves how to act, but we do not like to bear responsibility for our actions. We understand that our actions affect others, but we are angry or embarrassed when someone faces us with the need to admit our mistakes. "You were wrong" and "You sinned" are phrases that rouse our anger instead of moving us to self-examination and repentance.

We have great difficulty in accepting responsibility for our actions, so we try to hedge our apologies in all kinds of ways so as to reduce— even if just a little bit—the weight of our responsibility. That is not how Christians are called to live. That is not what we have learned from the gospel about sin and the way to rid ourselves of it.

The sailors asked Jonah what they must do *so that the seas* would *stop shrieking* over them. They describe the storm in personal terms, as if it were a creature towering over them, threatening and frightening, shrieking in their ears. It was such a terrible storm that it seemed to have assumed personal qualities.

Furthermore, the author tells us that *the sea was becoming increasingly stormier.* In response to Jonah's sin and refusal to acknowledge it, the sea's fury continually increased. The sailors were used to dealing with storms, but since this storm was fueled by God's anger, all of their efforts would be ineffective. They could drop sails, cast more of the cargo overboard or do anything else in an attempt to ride out the storm, but all would be for nothing. From the moment the sailors and the passengers learned of Jonah's sin, they were partners to it until they acted to distance themselves from it and appease God's anger. So they had to act, and they asked Jonah, "What shall we do to you?"

Jonah must have been terribly afraid as he replied, "Lift me up and throw me into the sea and the sea will stop shrieking over you, because I know that because of me this great storm is upon you." Surely he had no hope of being rescued.

But, at last, Jonah was willing to accept responsibility and submit to punishment for what he had done. This is a fundamental gospel principle—recognition of sin and of the fact that our guilt renders us liable to punishment. Until a person understands his guilt in light of God's holiness and righteousness, he will be unable to recognize his need of forgiveness or salvation.

Jonah was a prophet of God, but he had no thought of repenting and seeking God's mercy for himself or for those with him in the ship. Jonah had no mercy for Nineveh; neither did he understand at this point that he could expect mercy from God. All he knew was that he had sinned and had to bear the punishment that was due him. Repentance would come only after God had conquered Jonah's heart with a display of his terrible anger, leading the prophet to cast himself on God's mercy. Even God's anger is an instrument of grace!

Jonah viewed things much as we should view them at the beginning of our journey toward Christ. This is not a complete view of the gospel, but it is a necessary one. Before we understand the magnitude of God's grace we need to understand the greatness of his anger and the weight of our sins. At this stage, we seldom hope for salvation. Instead, we are overwhelmed by the heavy burden of sin.

But God is kind, merciful, gentle and good. He does not leave us for long in such a state—after all, he is working to save us. God worked in Jonah's life to bring the prophet to rely on divine grace and to proclaim that grace to others. This is how he works in all of our hearts if we learn to recognize our sins.

The Scripture tells us that the soul who sins shall die (Ezek.18:4, ESV), and Jonah understood that it should be so unless he repented. But Jonah did not consider repenting at this stage. He was preoccupied with the burden of his sin. He knew that, through his disobedience, he had brought on the innocent crew and passengers a terrible disaster. He decided to own up to his responsibility and to make up for his actions through his own death. This is how he intended to relieve others of the consequences for a deed for which they were not responsible.

Our attitude to others—and to ourselves—often indicates the nature of our faith and the measure of our understanding of the grace of God. To truly know God's grace is to make it a part of our lives. Someone who has done this will also show toward others the same grace on which he relies. Whoever understands that he is forgiven by grace and supported by grace throughout the course of his life, will inevitably be gracious to others. He will forgive freely, just as he has been forgiven. If we are such persons, we will understand that unless we forgive others their sins toward us, our Father in heaven will not forgive us (Matt. 6:15).

In his mercy, God will not allow us to evade the guilt of our sin because the only way to be freed from it is not to deny but to confess it, and then to cast it on the broad shoulders of God's grace—and we know more today of that grace than Jonah could have ever known because we have learned about grace from Jesus.

God desires our salvation, just as he wanted Jonah's salvation and, through it, the salvation of Nineveh. He is willing to shake heaven and earth, to raise storms and to stir terror in our hearts, in order to bring us to repentance and salvation.

There is nothing God will not do to save those he loves! This is worth remembering, especially when God's hand is heavy on us and we sense his anger—because his anger is designed to lead us to his grace. Recognition of this truth can comfort and encourage us; it can provide us with the strength to repent and to trust in him. God does not change. If we are saved by his grace, he will never be our enemy. He will always act to bless us, even if the blessing is hidden, wrapped in heavy storm clouds because of our failures.

Unexpected Grace—Verses 13–15

Jonah had said, "Lift me up and throw me into the sea." The sailors' response is surprising: "But the people rowed to return to the dry land, but could not because the sea was increasingly stormier against them." Jonah had brought on them a terrible disaster. The ship's cargo was lost, and with it all hope of profit—which could mean financial ruin. More urgently, everyone on board the ship remained in mortal danger.

Jonah had behaved with absolute moral indifference when he involved the others in his rebellion against God. He displayed his indifference further by going to sleep while the others fought for their lives. He did not even trouble himself to pray.

Now, discovered in spite of his efforts and after being forced to confess his guilt, he is shown mercy by the passengers and sailors. They do not throw him into the sea as he had suggested, and as he well deserved. Instead, they showed him kindness in the teeth of the threatening dangers—more kindness than Jonah had shown to them. *The people rowed to return to the dry land.* They tried, somehow, to rescue themselves and him as well.

In Romans 2:14–15, the apostle Paul speaks of the Gentiles, "who do not have the law, [yet] do by nature things required by the law." He says that "they are a law for themselves even though they do not have the law, since they show that the requirements of the law are written on their hearts, their consciences also bearing witness, and their thoughts now accusing, now even defending them."

His words remind us that all people are created in the image of God. In spite of sin and the distorted religions and worldviews that humankind has developed, something of the divine image remains in them all. That is why we sometimes find those who neither know God nor serve him behaving more morally than believers. Because of this, we must take care not to despise those who do not share our faith. We should not dare to think we are better than they are, for we often have a great deal to learn from those who do not live for God. A donkey taught the prophet Balaam, and here we see idol worshipers acting according to biblical moral principles—in direct contrast with Jonah's behavior, even though he was an Israelite and a prophet.

The people rowed to return to the dry land, but could not because the sea was increasingly stormier against them. Jonah the prophet of God neglected to pray; the sailors, who worshiped idols, prayed. When all hope was lost, when no other course seemed open, the sailors and the passengers "cried out to the Lord and said, 'Please, Lord, let us not perish because of the death of this man and do not hold us accountable for the death of an innocent, because you, O Lord, have done what you wished.' And they lifted Jonah and threw him into the sea."

Jonah had tried to escape God. But he was forced to stand before God in judgment.

There is no doubt that Jonah expected to die, drowning in the stormy sea. That is what the sailors thought. It is worth noting that they did not describe Jonah's expected drowning as *the death of an innocent* because they thought Jonah had done nothing wrong, but because they feared that his death at their hands was not the punishment that he deserved.

They go on to admit that *you, O Lord, have done what you wished.* That is the right way to think of the God of Israel: he rules over everything, his will is carried out in every event and circumstance. His will should be done in us and in heaven. We should be taken up with his will.

Back to Normal—Verse 16

The wind and the waves of the sea obey his command thoughtlessly, without having any choice in the matter. The sailors executed God's will reluctantly, with a very limited understanding of his greatness. We, who have been given the privilege to know so much about his grace and glory, should surely obey him with loving exuberance.

Immediately after they threw Jonah into the sea, "the sea's anger was relaxed. And the people greatly feared the Lord, so they offered the Lord a sacrifice and made vows to him." Suddenly, the sea was angry no more. All the forces of nature united in support of their divine Maker's quarrel with his rebellious prophet. Finally, Jonah bore his punishment and, as a result, the order of nature returned to its natural course.

After all, it is unimaginable that a man who refuses to obey God can escape punishment. This would be contrary to all logic. Impossible! So it is no surprise that the author describes the response of the wind and of the sea in personal terms. The foundations of the universe were shaken by Jonah's refusal to do what God had commanded him. Now that Jonah has borne the just consequences of his refusal, everything reverted to its natural course. The moon traversed the heavens, the sun returned to shine, the sea was calm and the wind ceased to blow.

The God who can hurl mighty winds onto the sea is also capable of calming them, as Christ demonstrated so many years later when he commanded the sea, *Be quiet!* And everything suddenly grew calm, echoing the words of Psalm 107:23–30:

> Others went out on the sea in ships; they were merchants on the mighty waters. They saw the works of the LORD, his wonderful deeds in the deep. He spoke and stirred up a tempest that lifted high the waves. They mounted up to the heavens and went down to the depths; in their peril their courage melted away. They reeled and staggered like drunken men; they were at their wits' end. Then they cried out to the LORD in their trouble, and he brought them out of their distress. He stilled the storm to a whisper; the waves of the sea were hushed. They were glad when it grew calm, and he guided them to their desired haven.

In light of this revelation of God's sovereignty, "the people greatly feared the Lord, so they offered the Lord a sacrifice and made vows to him." The sailors feared God in practical terms, while Jonah feared God only in theory. His lack of real fear expressed itself in his refusal to obey God's command. Jesus said that if we love him, we will keep his commandments. No one who refuses to obey can claim that he fears God as he ought to fear him, with love and reverence and awe. God is not interested in religious people who come to his temple and offer sacrifices, but in those whose love for and fear of him will motivate them to obey him eagerly.

The people greatly feared the Lord, so they offered the Lord a sacrifice and made vows to him. God was glorified through the punishment meted out to his rebellious servant. Everything the Lord does is meant to glorify his holy name. He is as glorified through his righteousness as he is through his grace.

No one can come before God with the complaint that he has suffered more than is his due, even if the motives of those who caused him pain were impure or that the specific suffering he endured was not in direct and appropriate response to his deeds. In the final run, every instance of suffering is meant either to punish or to sanctify, and there is not a human in the world that does not deserve to be punished, or that does not need to be sanctified. In Jonah's case, God glorified himself by having the prophet thrown into the raging sea, and the sea immediately ceased its raging.

The sailors and the passengers were unlikely to have turned to the Lord of Israel with a pure and well-informed faith. But they had learned something about God's glory that every human should know. In this, however unintentionally, Jonah was an instrument in God's hand to show idol worshipers his divine glory.

The story so far has all the elements of what we call a "testominy": a marvelous revelation from God, blatant sin, thrilling action, the grace of God, wonderful miracles and the recognition of sin. What follows does not present Jonah in the most favorable light. But the Scriptures are not designed to move us with wonderful stories of spiritual adventure. They are designed to teach us to think rightly about God so that we will live rightly and so that we relate to the Lord with the appropriate and loving reverence he deserves.

That is why the story does not end here. Instead, all we have learned is but an introduction to the main point, presented in the following chapters.

Summary

1. There is no way to escape from the Lord. He rules the affairs of this world with moral logic, and those who refuse to serve him willingly will do so unwillingly. All the powers of nature are united in doing God's will, and if we oppose God, he may cause them to rise against us.

2. God by his grace has called us to acknowledge our responsibility for all our actions. If we do so and confess our sins, he is just and faithful to forgive us all our sins and to cleanse us from all unrighteousness.

3. Our actions affect others; we are forbidden to be morally indifferent and to ignore that fact. Parents' actions affect their children, employees' their colleagues, believers' each other and the general health of the church. We must be very careful in the conduct of our lives, so that we bring good to others, not disaster.

4. The sailors were not hasty in casting Jonah into the sea although he had caused them so much damage. We often find that those who do not know God and do not serve him still show more than a bit of the image of God through honesty and kindness. We should learn from them to be like God and to lead lives that are pleasing to him.

Let's learn from God to forgive, and let us forgive each other with the same liberality that he forgives us. Let us praise the name of the Lord and live for his glory.

Prayer

You rule over all
and everything that exists does your will.
May your kingdom come,
may your will be done on earth as it is done in heaven,
in us and through us as through all mankind.
Teach us to love your will
and to do it from the depths of our hearts,
in the name of your Son, Jesus, Amen.

Questions for Discussion

1. How should we handle guilt? Where did Jonah err in this regard?

2. What have you learned about grace?

3. What have you learned about God's control of all things?

4

The Prophet Repents

1:17—2:10

The Lord appointed a large fish to swallow Jonah, and Jonah was in the belly of the fish three days and three nights. And Jonah prayed to the Lord his God from the belly of the fish and said, "I called out from my distress to the Lord and he answered me, from the depths of the grave I called out, you heard my voice.

"But you have cast me into the deep, in the heart of the oceans and a torrent surrounds me; all your breakers and your waves have passed over me. I said, 'I have been dispelled from your presence,' but I will keep looking toward your holy sanctuary.

"Waters have covered me to the point of death, the grave surrounds me, reeds are strapped around my head. I have gone down to the ends of mountains, the earth has shut its bolts above me forever—and you brought my life up out of corruption, my Lord, my God! When

*my soul was depressed within me, I remembered the
Lord and my prayer came to you, to your holy sanctuary.*

*"Those who regard empty vanities forsake their own
grace. As for me—I will sacrifice to you with the voice
of thanksgiving. I will pay what I have vowed. Salvation
is the Lord's!"*

*And the Lord commanded the fish, and it vomited
Jonah onto dry ground.*

Chapter 2 of Jonah's story naturally divides into five parts: in verses
1–3 Jonah remembers the past. In verses 4–7a the prophet describes
his situation. Verses 7b–8 express Jonah's hope. Verse 9 describes
Jonah's conclusions, and verse 10 tells us how God responded to the
prophet's prayer.

Jonah's prayer, which makes up the bulk of this section, is special
for a number of reasons. First, Jonah was apparently the only one
of the ship's passengers who had not prayed during the storm. He,
who avoided praying, now shows himself to be a master of prayer.
Like driving, prayer is learned through practice. From this prayer
it is clear that Jonah normally prayed a great deal more than we
might have thought.

There are times when we avoid praying, or pray little. Usually,
these are times of rebellion, when we desire to distance ourselves
from God lest our conscience trouble us. This was certainly true
of Jonah. He feared the Lord and knew him well but, at this point
in his life, he did not live as God would have him live, and did not
obey his command. The lack of obedience expressed itself in the
impoverishment of Jonah's spiritual life.

But God in his grace did not give up on Jonah. He pursued him
with a storm, with the ship's crew, and with an enormous fish—all
to cause Jonah to turn back to God and pray.

Second, Jonah's prayer is special because it is largely based on passages from the Psalms. Some sentences are direct quotes; others are

allusions. Jonah had apparently memorized the Scriptures, making them part of his intimate spiritual possession. From this prayer we can learn how to use the Scriptures and how to make what they say a part of our own spiritual possessions.

Compare these quotes from Jonah's prayer and the corresponding passages from the Psalms:

> *I called out from my distress to the Lord and he answered me.*

Compare with Psalm 120:1

> I call on the LORD in my distress and he answers me.

> *You have cast me into the deep, in the heart of the oceans and a torrent surrounds me; all your breakers and your waves have passed over me.*

Compare with Psalm 69: 2, 15

> I sink in the miry depths where there is no foothold. . . . I have come into the deep waters; the floods engulf me . . . Do not let the floodwaters engulf me or the depths swallow me up or the pit close its mouth over me.

> *I said, "I have been dispelled from your presence."*

Compare with Psalm 31:22

> In my alarm I said, "I am cut off from your sight!" Yet you heard my cry for mercy when I called to you for help.

> *I will keep looking toward your holy sanctuary.*

Compare with Psalm 5:7

> I, by your great mercy, will come into your house; in reverence will I bow down toward your holy temple

and Psalm 138:2

I will bow down toward your holy temple and will praise your name for your love and your faithfulness, for you have exalted above all things your name and your word.

Waters have covered me to the point of death, the grave surrounds me, reeds are strapped around my head. I have gone down to the ends of mountains; the earth has shut its bolts above me forever.

Compare with Psalm 18:4–5

The cords of death entangled me; the torrents of destruction overwhelmed me. The cords of the grave coiled around me, the snares of death confronted me.

Compare with Psalm 69:2

I sink in the miry depths, where there is no foothold. I have come into the deep waters, the floods engulf me.

and with Psalm 116:3

The cords of death entangled me; the anguish of the grave came upon me. I was overcome by trouble and sorrow.

You brought my life up out of corruption, my Lord, my God!

Compare with Psalm 30:1, 3

I will exalt you, O LORD, for you lifted me out of the depths and did not let my enemies gloat over me. O LORD my God, I called to you for help and you healed me. O LORD, you brought me up from the grave.

Those who regard empty vanities.

Compare with Psalm 31:6

I hate those who cling to worthless idols, I trust in the LORD.

As for me—I will sacrifice to you with the voice of thanksgiving.

Compare with Psalm 116:17

I will sacrifice a thank offering to you and call on the name of the LORD.

I will pay what I have vowed.

Compare with Psalm 54:6

I will sacrifice a freewill offering to you, I will praise your name, O LORD

Compare with Psalm 66:13 KJV

I will go into thy house with burnt offerings: I will pay thee my vows

and with Psalm 116:14, 18 KJV

I will pay my vows unto the LORD now.

Salvation is the Lord's!

Compare with Psalm 3:8

From the LORD comes deliverance.

(salvation—in Hebrew the identical phrase appears in Jonah and in Psalms with the words reversed).

The third reason why Jonah's prayer is so special is that he prayed under extremely difficult circumstances. His death seemed certain, with no hope of rescue, and yet he prayed. He knew it was wise to pray because there is nothing God cannot do. Even when our situation is desperate, even when it seems that we're in the belly of a fish, we are not beyond the reach of God's mighty hand.

Finally, Jonah's prayer is special because even though Jonah turned his back on God, God did not turn his back on Jonah. God pursued Jonah until he overpowered him and brought him back to himself. Jonah prayed knowing he was guilty of sinning against the Lord. Apparently, he knew God to be a God of mercy and of grace (although he did not want that grace to be shown toward others). Jonah did not despair even though he had rebelled against God by defying God's command. We are never beyond the reach of God's grace, and Jonah teaches us that we should always trust him and pray to him.

Jonah Remembers the Past—Verses 1–3

"The Lord appointed a large fish to swallow Jonah, and Jonah was in the belly of the fish three days and three nights. And Jonah prayed to the Lord his God from the belly of the fish and said, 'I called out from my distress to the Lord and he answered me, from the depths of the grave I called out, you heard my voice.'"

Three days and three nights had passed since the terrifying moment when Jonah was thrown into the sea and swallowed by the fish. Try to imagine how you would have felt. Think of the horror that would have gripped you as the sailors begin to whisper among themselves, throwing furtive glances in your direction. Then they turn and approach you, grim and determined. They seize you and throw you overboard into the sea! The cold, salty waves crash over you. Suddenly an enormous fish appears, opens its mouth and swallows you with a single gulp. You are frightened out of your wits. In the darkness, a paralyzing despair takes hold of you—a despair that Jonah describes in his prayer.

Three days and three nights in the belly of a fish! You wonder if you're dead. Slowly the terrible reality of your situation dawns on you: in spite of everything you expected when you were thrown overboard, you're still alive.

Hope begins to sprout. You recall how you heard God's command and fled, refusing to obey. You deserve to die without hope. Then you recall circumstances in the past, when God acted in wonderful ways in spite of your sins and of the seemingly insurmountable difficulties you then faced. You examine your heart. You remember that, as long as there is a God in heaven, there are solid grounds for hope. There is no limit to his power or to his grace. So you call out to him.

And Jonah prayed to the Lord his God from the belly of the fish.

Jonah first encouraged his heart and, at the same time, reminded God of his grace. There were somewhat similar situations in the past: difficult, impossible, and desperate. But Jonah says, "I called out from my distress to the Lord and he answered me, from the depths of the grave I called out, you heard my voice." Once before he saw himself as good as dead, in *the depths of the grave*, just as he sees himself now. But then he *called out from [his] distress to the Lord and he answered*. He heard Jonah's previous prayer and responded; he listened to Jonah's cry in spite of his sin *and answered*. God saved Jonah then; might he not save him now?

Sisters and brothers, it does not matter how much you have sinned and rebelled against God. He is a forgiving God. It does not matter how difficult your circumstances might be, for there are no circumstances over which God is powerless and which he cannot change.

Even if you're in the depths of the grave, God can change things. He raises the dead. He made heaven and earth and everything they contain with a single, short command (one word in Hebrew): "Let there be." He tore the sea in two and shook the earth—the same earth that revolves around the sun at his command. It was he who appointed the fish to swallow Jonah—all creatures fulfill his will—and he also appointed your trials. Be helped by them. Learn from them to trust in and rely on God, and to turn to him in all circumstances.

Make use of the past also, as Jonah did when he reminded himself: "I called out from my distress to the Lord and he answered me, from the depths of the grave I called out, you heard my voice." Encourage yourself with memories of what God has done. The past is there so that we can learn from it—so that we can stand on its shoulders in the present and stretch out our hand to the future, toward God, hope, and salvation. Believe! Trust God! Don't believe the lies that circumstances whisper in your ear, the hopeless deceptions of your heart. Trust like Jonah did, hoping against hope. If you rely on God, you will never be disappointed.

Jonah's Difficult Situation—Verses 4–7a

Next, Jonah turned from his memories to his circumstances. He reminded himself how he got into his predicament and described the struggle that raged in his heart: "You have cast me into the deep, in the heart of the oceans and a torrent surrounds me; all your breakers and your waves have passed over me. I said, 'I have been dispelled from your presence, but I will keep looking toward your holy sanctuary.' Waters have covered me to the point of death, the grave surrounds me, reeds are strapped around my head."

It was not a coincidence that Jonah found himself in the belly of a fish; it was an act of God. That is why Jonah says *you have cast me*. He acknowledges that God brought him into this situation, not the sailors or anyone else. Ultimately, all that exists executes God's will, even if they are unwitting and unwilling. Jonah was not in the hands of chance or blind fate. He was in God's hands. This gave sense to these events, and he admitted that God is the Master who wisely and rationally governed the details of his life. The breakers that crashed onto the deck of the ship and the waves that broke on his head were *your breakers and your waves*. They did God's will. They were created by God's command.

Here is a wonderful basis for hope! Sisters and brothers, in times of crisis and pain, draw near to God. Examine your hearts and your lives. Ask what lesson you are to learn from this trial. Remember, like Jonah, that you are not in the hand of blind fate. You are not victims of a coincidence. God rules over all the details and difficulties of your lives. They all serve God's purpose, and his purposes are always good, worthy and acceptable. Don't give in to bitterness, which is a form of rebellion that will drive you further from God and increase your pain. Trust in God and in his wonderful grace. Respond with a moral wisdom that is motivated by spiritual assumptions. Act according to the Scriptures, and remember that the first thing you must do is trust God.

Circumstances might be tough. They might provoke you to despair. Don't give in. Again: don't listen to the circumstances; listen to God, who has promised "I will never leave you nor forsake you" (Joshua 1:5). God supports those who fail. He defends the widows and the orphans. His heart is kind and soft toward you if you are in Christ. If you are not—turn quickly to him, and find in him safety and peace.

Having described his circumstances, Jonah now describes his feeling when he woke up in the belly of the fish and realized that he was alive, but with no visible hope of rescue. "I said, 'I have been dispelled from your presence.'" The first thought that came to his mind was a terrible one: "I'm done for. God has cast me out of his sight and will no longer pay any attention to me. He will no longer watch over me. He will not save me." To someone who has tasted God's goodness and learned to rely on it in his daily life, no thought could be worse than to think that his access to grace had been barred by sin.

Deep in his heart, Jonah knew that this was impossible. The God of Israel, the covenant-making God who retains his grace to a thousand generations, is not that kind of a God. He loves to be kind. He loves to forgive. He loves to love. So Jonah quickly dismissed this first mistaken, atheistic thought. He hastened to add, "I said, 'I have been dispelled from your presence—but I will keep looking toward your holy sanctuary.'"

It is as if he says, "In spite of what my circumstances might be telling me, in spite of the despairing whispers of my sinful heart and in spite of the awareness of sin that grips me, I will keep looking toward your holy sanctuary just like my forefathers did when they sinned against you and, when Moses raised the bronze serpent, they looked toward it in faith and expectation. All who looked in faith were healed. That's how I will look toward your holy sanctuary.

I will not rely on my labors as a prophet in your service. I won't boast about any spiritual exploits as if I could trust in them. *I will keep looking toward your holy sanctuary*, where sacrifices for sin are offered according to your commandment, where your people serve you according to your word. There sinners are atoned for and obtain forgiveness."

That is why Jonah mentioned the sanctuary—the temple. He knew that Israel's sacrifices for sin were offered there, and he relied on those sacrifices. The most important part of the temple service was the offering of atoning sacrifices.

The people of Israel did not come into the temple to worship; they stood outside and had no active part in the worship of God. Apart from bringing sacrifices and handing them over to the priests, they did nothing. They were not allowed to approach the altar, or enter the court where the sacrifices were made. They certainly did not see the hall with the table of showbread and the altar of incense, lit by the candelabra's faint light. They could not draw near to the Holy of Holies, move the curtain and peer through the darkness to see the ark of the covenant, on which was the mercy seat where the high priest annually sprinkled blood on the Day of Atonement.

The sacrifices were the main feature in the temple, and that is what Jonah referred to when he said *I will keep looking toward your holy sanctuary*. "I refuse to despair," he says. "I refuse to give in to unbelief. I refuse to listen to anything but God's promises to forgive, epitomized in the temple."

He relied here on the same expectation that Solomon expressed when he prayed, "May your eyes be open toward this temple night and day, this place of which you said, 'My Name shall be there,' so that you will hear the prayer your servant prays toward this place. Hear the supplication of your servant and of your people Israel when they pray toward this place. Hear from heaven, your dwelling place, and when you hear, forgive" (1 Kings 8:29–30).

Then Jonah returned to his difficult situation: "Waters have covered me to the point of death, the grave surrounds me, reeds are strapped around my head. I have gone down to the ends of mountains, the earth has shut its bolts above me forever." This is a description of what happened to him in the fish's belly, combining external details with his thoughts.

Waters have covered me to the point of death. Sea water and digestive fluids threatened to drown him. *The grave surrounds me.* The darkness, the strange sounds, the stench and the waters made the prophet think he had descended to the dwelling place of the dead.

Reeds are strapped around my head The fish swallowed everything in its path, including seaweeds and other marine vegetation. These wrapped themselves around the prophet's head as he lay helpless in the fish's stomach. There in the darkness, he felt as if he had *gone down to the ends of mountains,* to the very depths of the earth and *the earth has shut its bolts above me forever.* In those days the earth was thought to be a well-guarded grave from which none could rise, a prison from which there was no escape once the bolts of earth's doors were shut.

Torn between hope and fear, between encouraging memories and unimaginably terrifying circumstances, the prophet turned to God.

Jonah's Hope—Verses 7b–8

> And you brought my life up out of corruption, my Lord, my God! When my soul was depressed within me, I remembered the Lord and my prayer came to you, to your holy sanctuary.
>
> "Those who regard empty vanities forsake their own grace. As for me—I will sacrifice to you with the voice of thanksgiving. I will pay what I have vowed. Salvation is the Lord's!"
>
> And the Lord commanded the fish, and it vomited Jonah onto dry ground.

We've already heard something of Jonah's hope. It is to this hope that he returns in these verses.

This is a good example of how the past serves us. Jonah encouraged himself with the memory of the past, using it to move his heart to trust. In the past, God heard his prayer, and this gives Jonah confidence that God will certainly hear him again.

It is wonderful that God would listen to our prayers. Why should he? Who are we that we deserve such attention from him? We are no more than dust and ashes—yet the Scriptures teach otherwise. While they describe us as dust and ashes, they also teach that God attributes great value to us. We are created in his image, for his glory and praise, and for the accomplishment of his will. The Scriptures teach that God listens to and answers our prayers! (Ps. 65:2).

Another, still more amazing truth is that God even hears the prayers of those who have sinned against him, just as he heard Jonah's prayer. That is an excellent reason to pray, to turn to God and love him in your prayers. It is a wonderful reason to share with him the most intimate, most important things of our lives. It is good to talk to someone who knows how to listen. How much better it is to speak to God, who always listens with interest and love!

Jonah added an important detail to his prayer. He addressed God as *my Lord, my God* (v. 6). Jonah's God is not a foreign, distant God. He is the God *of Jonah*, the God of the covenant with Jonah, the God of the grace that was given Jonah. He is the God of Jonah's life and heart, in spite of his disobedience and rebellion. Do you know God in this way? If you do, you will undoubtedly pray to him often.

Jonah's Conclusions—Verses 9–10

In light of all this, Jonah came to a conclusion that influenced his perspective on life: "Those who regard empty vanities forsake their own grace. As for me—I will sacrifice to you with the voice of thanksgiving. I will pay what I have vowed. Salvation is the Lord's!" *Empty vanities* are beliefs that idols have any power to help us; that deny God; that believe in human effort rather than in the mercy of God; and that avoid relying on God as he is revealed in the Scriptures.

Those who regard empty vanities are those who know the Lord—as Jonah knew him—yet forsake his ways.

Beware of any tendency to stray from the ways of God. Those who stray *forsake their own grace.* They abandon the foundation that can make sense and bring lasting good out of life, the only possible basis for a relationship with God. Grace! That is what we need, not justice, but something far beyond what we deserve.

This view goes against our normal ways of thinking. We like to think that we deserve everything— happiness, respect, love and reasonable economic security if not prosperity. We tend to assume that God is duty-bound to listen to our prayers and that he will be impressed with our religious performance. We always need Jonah's reminder: *Those who regard empty vanities forsake their own grace.* Grace is what we need.

Remembering this, Jonah decided to act in a way that contradicted his previous behavior. "As for me [in contrast with those who regard empty vanities]—I will sacrifice to you with the voice of thanksgiving. I will pay what I have vowed. Salvation is the Lord's!" Jonah repented. He submitted to the will of God. He undertook to conduct his life with honest gratitude to God for his grace; therefore in obedience to his commandments he says, *I will pay what I have vowed.*

Jonah's rebellion was put down. God took action and made Jonah submit to him. As we will see, this did not make Jonah perfect; he still had a good deal to learn about God and about his ways. But, at this stage, his rebellion came to an end.

Who says that God does not force us to obey him? When he wants to, he forces his will on us. Note what he did to bring Jonah to obey him. Don't fight God. Do his will happily, lovingly, and don't force him to force you.

A central part of repentance is a willingness to submit to God, just as a central part of sin is a refusal to submit to God's authority in our lives. It is impossible to repent and, at the same time, continue to consider ourselves masters of our lives. The mere fact that we ask God to save us is an admission of his sovereignty. Anyone who wants God to be his savior must first of all crown him king of his life and heart.

Can you remember when you repented? Can you remember your first days in Christ, the promises you made to God? "Lord, I'll serve you at any price. I will faithfully do whatever you wish. I'll pray often. I'll study Scripture faithfully. I'll be more than faithful in church life. I'll deny myself daily, give you all that I have and follow your Son, Jesus."

Have you made such promises? Are you fulfilling those promises? Are you truly devoted to God, serving in the church as best you can with your abilities, time and finances, denying yourselves in cases of disagreement with a fellow believer? Do you love God as you have promised to love him? Do you offer hospitality with heart-warming generosity and enthusiasm? Do you care for the sick, the lonely and the weak?

Where is your first love? Where is your enthusiasm for contemplating God's will? Where is the passion that characterized you, when you took part in congregational activities, shared in every event, contributed as much as you could, prayed and listened attentively to every sermon?

Beloved, vows ought to be fulfilled. "Those who regard empty vanities forsake their own grace. As for me—I will sacrifice to you with the voice of thanksgiving. I will pay what I have vowed." Will you return to your first love? Or will you prefer to be lukewarm, neither hot nor cold, neither committed nor in denial, not devoted but not quite withdrawn from congregational life? Jonah insisted, *Those who regard empty vanities forsake their own grace. As for me—I will sacrifice to you with the voice of thanksgiving. I will pay what I have vowed.* Will you say as much, now, at this very moment before God?

God brought Jonah to the point where the prophet was willing to obey. He would go to Nineveh. He would declare God's word to the city.

What does God need to do in our lives to bring us to the point of obedience?

The Lord Responds to the Prophet's Prayer—Verse 11

Jonah prayed *and the Lord commanded the fish, and it vomited Jonah onto dry ground*. The Master of all creation accomplished all he wanted, and therefore commanded the fish, which spat Jonah out onto dry ground.

Summary

1. There is wisdom in prayer. We can pray to God, and we have good reasons to do so. God hears prayer and invites us to turn to him.

2. Learn from the past to equip yourself for the present and the future. In particular, remember God's grace. Rely on that grace every time you face a difficulty.

3. We can never go beyond the reach of God's grace. God can overrule every situation. He can overcome any and all of our sins.

4. Do not rely on anyone or anything but God. Turn to him and be saved. *Those who regard empty vanities forsake their own grace.* Trust in God, in him alone.

Prayer

God of the heavens and of the earth,
God of mercy and of grace,
who invites sinners to turn to him and be saved,
we turn to you,
please save us, forgive us our sins and teach us to trust you,
in the name of your Son, Jesus, Amen.

Questions for Discussion

1. Define true repentance.

2. How do the issues of guilt, accountability, divine grace and repentance figure in Jonah's prayer? What does that teach you?

3. What is the role of the Word of God in faith and in prayer?

4. How should we use past experiences?

5. What were the grounds of Jonah's hope? How are these expressed in your faith and life?

6. What have you learned about prayer?

5

Jonah Prophesies in Nineveh

3:1–5

And the word of the Lord came to Jonah for the second time, saying, "Get up, go to Nineveh, that great city, and declare to her what I am saying to you." So Jonah got up and went to Nineveh according to the command of the Lord.

Now Nineveh was a very big city, a walk of three days. And Jonah began entering the city for a day's walk and declared, saying, "Forty more days and Nineveh is destroyed!"

The people of Nineveh believed in God, and declared a fast and wore sackcloth, from the greatest to the least of them.

(vv. 6–10) The matter had been heard by the king of Nineveh, so he arose from his throne, removed his kingly robe, covered himself with sackcloth and sat on the ashes. He also summoned and said, "In Nineveh,

on behalf of the king and his nobles: Man and beast,
the cattle and the sheep, are not to taste anything, not
to pasture and not to drink water. They are to cover
themselves with sackcloth—man and beast—and call
mightily out to God and return each from his evil way
and from the (gains of the) violent robbery he has done.
Who knows, God may change his mind and repent of his
anger, and we will not perish."

And the Lord saw from their deeds that they had
turned from their evil ways, and the Lord repented of
the evil he had said he would do to them, and did not
do it.

Jonah Obeys—Verses 1–3a

It all began when the Lord said to Jonah, "Get up, go to Nineveh, that great city, and call out against her because their evil has come up before me." People must do what God tells them to do, and that is certainly true of his messengers, the prophets. Jonah tried to escape his duty, but there is no escape from God. He fills the heavens and the earth, and there is no place in the heavens, on earth or under the earth where we can hide from him.

The will of God *will* be carried out—inevitably!—and so we are back at square one. The author uses very similar language here as he did in the opening of chapter 1. The similarity serves to teach us, the readers, that God brought Jonah back to the point where it all began, and that God stubbornly insisted, refusing to let go until his will was done.

The book begins with the words, "The word of the Lord came to Jonah the son of Amitai: 'Get up, go to Nineveh, that great city, and call out against her because their evil has come up before me.' And Jonah got up, to flee to Tarshish from the presence of the Lord." It continues in this chapter with the words, "and the word of the Lord came to Jonah for the second time, saying, 'Get up, go to Nineveh, that great city, and declare to her what I am saying to you.' So Jonah got up and went to Nineveh according to the command of the Lord."

The author wanted to emphasize that this was the second time that the Lord had addressed Jonah, with almost the same message. He makes a point of indicating this by using the same language twice —with important differences.

In the first call, Jonah was instructed to *call out against* Nineveh. This time he is told to *declare to her*—a substantial difference that provides a hint of the grace God intended to show the Ninevites— exactly as Jonah feared.

Furthermore, in the first call the Lord told him to call out against the inhabitants of the city *because their evil* had come up before the Lord. Now he is sharply cautioned, *Declare to her what I am saying to you*. He is neither to add nor to subtract from the message the Lord will give him.

Declare to her although you refused to do that earlier. *Declare to her what I am saying to you*—nothing more, nothing less. Say what I say. Be faithful. Be careful in what you say. Obey because you are not your own messenger but a messenger of God.

That is how preachers should preach, evangelists should evangelize and believers should believe: according to the Word of God, no more and no less. We should not think that we can make the gospel more attractive or effective by our additions. We should not think that we can make the gospel more compelling by our omissions. It is our duty to declare, believe and live by the whole counsel of God—with no changes.

The message God committed to Jonah was greater than Jonah himself—and such is the case with all who teach the Word of God. Without doubt, we must demand of those who teach us to exert themselves, to sacrifice and to grow in their spiritual and moral qualities, but we must also always remember that the truth they declare is greater than them by far. The divine message is better than its human messenger, and the messenger must remain faithful to the message.

This brings us to a significant event in the narrative. In chapter 1 we read that Jonah heard the word of the Lord, "and Jonah got up, to flee to Tarshish from the presence of the Lord." This time we read, *So Jonah got up*—not to escape as he did in the past—*and went to Nineveh according to the command of the Lord.* In both instances the author describes him as "getting up," but in the first instance he got up to flee in disobedience. This time he got up *and went to Nineveh.* The author emphasizes that the prophet acted in this case *according to the command of the Lord.* At long last the prophet obeyed!

Following his unsuccessful rebellion, Jonah obeyed the Lord and turned in obedience to Nineveh. God himself created this difference in the prophet's heart. He changed the inclination of Jonah's will and made it bend toward his command. That is what we should ask for ourselves: "Bend my heart toward your word" (Ps. 119:36). In other words, drive sin from my thoughts, teach me to prefer your honor to mine, your will to my will and your kingdom more than anything else. Give me the grace that will enable me to first seek your kingdom and righteousness, to deny myself, to love you more than all else and to prefer you to my family, welfare and even my life.

We ought to be careful with such a prayer, especially when we remember what was involved in changing Jonah's heart! We often need a work of God in our hearts, a work no less radical than the one Jonah underwent, so that our hearts will submit to the will of our Creator and so that we will learn to love what he loves.

Jonah needed to learn a good deal about the ways of God, and that is the point of the story. It was written under inspiration of the Spirit of God and preserved in holy Scripture because we all have a similar need. If we do not learn to recognize and deal with it through Jonah's story, God will have to act to teach us, as he did for Jonah. What must God do in *your* life so that you will carry out his good, perfect and acceptable will?

God loves us. He wants the best for us. He wants us to be blessed, happy, holy and at peace with him and with all mankind. But this "best," this blessing, has to do with us following his will and tuning our hearts to his.

For this reason, God wants us to learn to do his will with enthusiasm, love and willingness. This is an important lesson from the book of Jonah, and I hope we will all learn it. Love God! Love his will! Direct your hearts to his will. If need be—and I think we often are in need of this—change your heart. Ask God to change it. And above all else, prefer the will of God.

Sometimes preachers who focus on explaining the word of God before applying it are asked, "Why don't you preach more practical sermons? Why don't you tell us how we should act in certain situations, and how to respond to specific circumstances?"

I'm confident that you do not want preachers to think for you, to make your life decisions. Preachers are not the masters of your consciences and do not want to treat you as if you are children. You need to do your own thinking. You need to make decisions.

A preacher's job is not to give you instructions about how to act in given situations but to teach you the principles of the Scripture and the commandments of God. It is your job to understand these things, internalize them and apply them in the varying circumstances of your life. What can be more practical, then, than the call to prefer God's will to our own? Exactly how that should be carried out in your life is a matter between you and God, the Master of your lives and of your hearts.

We're very much involved in practical issues, but in the way the Scripture deals with them. God did not provide us with a manual, a checklist of what to do and what not to do for given situations. He gave us sixty-six books that require study, examination, research, analysis and thought. Through this process, with the help of the Spirit and the support of an obedient heart, we are supposed to come to decisions in the course of life.

That is what good preachers seek to do. They refuse to follow the example of those who prefer to tell their listeners in detail what to do, leaving no room for responsible consideration, increasing maturity and spiritual independence. Instead, they equip their congregations for Christian thinking and decision making.

Prefer the will of God; that is the lesson we learn here. How this principle should be applied is for each of us to determine in our particular situations. We should also learn that we cannot do God's will unless he works in our hearts, moving us in that direction. That is why we must ask God to work in our hearts and lives, so that we will live as he wants us to live.

Jonah prophesies in Nineveh—Verses 3b–4

"Now Nineveh was a very big city, a walk of three days. And Jonah began entering the city for a day's walk and declared, saying, 'Forty more days and Nineveh is destroyed!'"

The expression *a walk of three days* apparently means that three full days were needed to walk through the whole of the city— its streets, temple and trade areas, and residential sections. Archeologists have explored the ruins of Nineveh and concluded that its circumference was about eight miles.

They estimate that up to 175,000 inhabitants lived in the city. Jonah 4:11 states that there were many more than 120,000 residents who could not tell their right hand from their left. It is possible this refers to the number of children in the city who were too young to know the difference between right and wrong. It is more likely that it refers to the total number of inhabitants, none of whom knew right from wrong because of their idolatrous culture and their lack of divine revelation.

Just like today, around each ancient city there were suburbs and slightly more distant townships—possibly up to 500,000, although the exact number is unknown. Such inhabited areas have been discovered along the Euphrates and Tigris rivers, on both sides, from the ruins of Nineveh to the northeast and the southwest. We do not know if the description of the city given in the book of Jonah only refers to the city or if it includes the city's larger environs. Either way, Nineveh was an exceptionally large city in comparison with most cities of its time.

"And Jonah began entering the city for a day's walk and declared, saying, 'Forty more days and Nineveh is destroyed!'"

The text uses an unusual term, "overturned," taken from the narrative of the destruction of Sodom (see Gen. 19:29). We should not assume that the Ninevites would have noticed this connection, but we should. Sodom and Gomorrah were destroyed because *the outcry to the LORD against its people* was *so great* (Gen. 19:13). So it was with the inhabitants of Nineveh. We have seen that the God of Israel is the Lord of all nations, and that he will call all of them to justice.

There is no clear call to repentance in Jonah's message, and no promise that if the city's residents repent, they will be forgiven. But these are implied by the mere fact that Jonah was sent to warn the Ninevites. After all, if all God intended was to destroy the city, Jonah would not have been sent to warn its inhabitants. If the Lord had not intended to be merciful to those who repent, he would not have instructed Jonah to convey any kind of message.

Words have meaning far beyond what they openly express. Their implications are often wider than we think or intend. That is why it is important that we be careful with what we say, that we learn to speak precisely and clearly about the Christian faith, and that we explore the wider implications of our assertions before we make them. Unintended implications take on life once the words are spoken. They may divert us and those who hear us from God's truth, even though we intend the opposite.

An excellent example of this can be found in the error Paul labored to correct in his letter to the Galatians. Those who came from Jerusalem merely wanted to teach the Galatians that they should keep the Law as given by God at Sinai. They were sincere Christians and certainly did not intend to deny the sufficiency of

Christ's atoning sacrifice. Nor did they intend to divide the church into those who were spiritual and those who were not. But these were the implications of their teachings. As a result, Paul was forced to insist that all who taught such things were cut off from Christ and from grace, and that they had departed from the faith because of their boast in their accomplishments instead of in the grace of God and the sacrifice of Messiah.

A capable teacher of the word of God is able to identify fine points and recognize the wider implications of both truth and error. That is one important way he protects himself and the flock he serves. This is one reason why it is so valuable to study theology. Theology equips us to identify implications, choose our words carefully, expose errors at their very outset and uproot them before they take root in the minds and hearts of Christian people.

Don't compromise in this matter. Those who teach us must be constantly engaged in the study of God's word, delving deeply into its message, into the theology of the text. We're not just interested in curiosities, psychological insights or exciting stories. These elements all make it easier for us to listen and understand, but only so long as they also invite us into a process of ever-deepening investigation of the spiritual and moral principles of God's word.

Jonah's words were sharp and clear: *"Forty more days and Nineveh is destroyed!"* But they were pregnant with meaning, and the Ninevites understood the implication. They drew the right conclusions, as we learn from what follows.

The Ninevites Respond—Verse 5

"The people of Nineveh believed in God, and declared a fast and wore sackcloth, from the greatest to the least of them."

Note, in response to the declaration of the word of God, *the people of Nineveh believed in God.* Their faith in God expressed itself in the way they related to his message. The Ninevites heard Jonah's words of warning, recognized the truth in them and responded to that truth appropriately.

They did not respond as we all are tempted to do when our sin is exposed and we are reminded of our deserved punishment—they were not angry. They did not insist that, had Jonah spoken more softly, more lovingly, they would have listened to him. They did not insist that he first come to encourage them, enhance their sense of dignity or serve their interests.

A stranger comes to town and all he has to say is, *"Forty more days and Nineveh is destroyed!"* Is that how a Christian behaves? Is that how someone talks if he loves his fellow human as he loves himself and really wants the other's happiness? What happened to kindness? Where is the delightful, comfortable, cozy sweetness that is assumed to be a primary Christian virtue today? Apparently, Jonah (like Peter, Paul and any of the apostles), had a very different view of the message that needed to be preached. He did not think that sweet gentleness is the primary Christian trait or that the love of God was his only characteristic. His message had teeth, a cutting edge, a real backbone!

Such was the message God commanded Jonah to deliver, and that was the message he delivered. There are times when there is no option but to threaten, to be sharp and firm. This, too, is an important aspect of the gospel. We are not to be men-pleasers but faithful servants of God, and in so doing we will best serve the true interests of those who hear us, even if it does not increase our popularity.

The Lord is not a soft-hearted granddad whose grandchildren are allowed to do whatever they wish. He is a holy, terrible God, a burning fire. His eyes are too pure to look at sin and he hates evil. We cannot faithfully preach the gospel without referring to that awful hatred.

Note, too, the wonderful result Jonah's "harsh" gospel brought: *The people of Nineveh believed in God, and declared a fast and wore sackcloth, from the greatest to the least of them.*

Beloved, gentleness can be cruel when it cloaks a timidity that hesitates to point to God's holiness and fears to describe man's sin in light of that holiness. On the other hand, what appears to be harshness can be—like the severing of a diseased limb—an act of necessary grace that saves the patient.

Let's not expect to come home from church every time in a happy, pleasant mood. We are all still sinful, so we should expect to go home at times embarrassed and distressed by the word of God. Our sins will have been exposed and our sense of our need for grace renewed. There are times when that is the form of grace we need.

Don't aim at a feel-happy gospel. Aim at truth, and give truth time to bear its fruit. Sometimes hours, days, even weeks will pass before we experience that peace which is the product of the Holy Spirit's work in our hearts, a peace that is based on the sacrifice of Messiah in the teeth of our sins. Meanwhile, we will ache, we will feel shame and pain, and we will cry out to God. Better a real conversion than a hasty one that might well be false. Better a pain that will drive us to God than a pleasant feeling that keeps us comfortable without him.

When did you last put on sackcloth after you heard the word of God? When was the last time that the word of God touched your heart and stirred it to an honest, radical response? Do you really listen to the sermons preached in your church? Do you examine yourself in light of what you hear? Do you prepare your heart before the service, in the hope that you will hear the voice of the living God?

The people of Nineveh believed in God, and declared a fast and wore sackcloth, from the greatest to the least of them. We should learn from the Ninevites to respond as warmly to God's word as they did.

Summary

1. God is a stubborn lover. He will bring us to do his will even if we resist him. He insists that his will be done, on earth as it is done in heaven.

2. God changes our hearts, and that is what we should be asking for every single day, so long as it is day, lest we stumble into sin.

3. We would do well to be careful with our words and our thoughts: they have implications that are often far wider than what may be obvious. It is important to think and to speak wisely, carefully and in accordance with the Scriptures. We expect at least as much from those who teach us.

4. The right way to believe in God is to trust his word and to obey it. A proper response to the word of God will radically shake and shape our lives, uproot habits and customary patterns. The word of God demands that we change, and if we believe the Scriptures we will undoubtedly change.

Prayer

God of all hearts and human souls,
you know our weaknesses and our sins.
Cleanse us of them by your grace and your mighty power.
Teach us to believe in you,
to love your word and to obey it
instead of seeking our own pleasures.
In the name of your Son Jesus, Amen.

Questions for Discussion

1. What is the difference between God's first command to Jonah and the second? How would you explain that difference?

2. What have you learned about preaching in general and about preaching the gospel in particular?

3. How should we view those who lead and serve us in the Lord?

4. Summarize what you have learned about the will of God in the world and in the lives of individuals.

6

Jonah Prophesies in Nineveh

3:6–10

And the word of the Lord came to Jonah for the second time, saying, "Get up, go to Nineveh, that great city, and declare to her what I am saying to you." So Jonah got up and went to Nineveh according to the command of the Lord.

Now Nineveh was a very big city, a walk of three days. And Jonah began entering the city for a day's walk and declared, saying, "Forty more days and Nineveh is destroyed!"

The people of Nineveh believed in God, and declared a fast and wore sackcloth, from the greatest to the least of them:

(vv. 6–10) The matter had been heard by the king of Nineveh, so he arose from his throne, removed his kingly robe, covered himself with sackcloth and sat on the ashes. He also summoned and said, "In Nineveh,

on behalf of the king and his nobles: Man and beast, the cattle and the sheep, are not to taste anything, not to pasture and not to drink water. They are to cover themselves with sackcloth—man and beast—and call mightily out to God and return each from his evil way and from the (gains of the) violent robbery he has done. Who knows, God may change his mind and repent of his anger, and we will not perish."

And the Lord saw from their deeds that they had turned from their evil ways, and the Lord repented of the evil he had said he would do to them, and did not do it.

Jonah arrived in the city and began to declare the word of God: *"Forty more days and Nineveh is destroyed!"* His words created a stir, and then a revolution: "The people of Nineveh believed in God, and declared a fast and wore sackcloth, from the greatest to the least of them."

At times, the Scriptures say "from the least to the greatest" (Jer. 31:34, for example). When they do so, there is a good reason— to include all, without distinction (although not necessarily without exception). In Nineveh's case, the point is slightly different. While *from the greatest to the least* certainly includes all the Ninevites without distinction, it emphasizes that the process of repentance began with the *greatest*. It began at the royal court, with the king and his nobles.

That is how things should be. Leaders are supposed to lead in spiritual and moral matters, although it is precisely those who lead that often find it most difficult to accept responsibility. It is hard to stand at the peak of the pyramid and admit your weaknesses. It is tough, when everyone's eyes are on you, not to hide your sins. But in Nineveh, repentance began *from the greatest* and proceeded *to the least of them.*

This should be the process in every context. Leaders and all who are looked up to need to set an example by leading others in the ways of God. They should be the first to accept criticism, the first to examine their ways, the first to admit their own faults and to correct them. A people, a church or a family will seldom be better than its leaders. Good leaders will strive for spiritual and moral perfection, and will seek purity of motive and action.

The King and His Nobles Repent—Verses 6–9

These verses expand on verse 5, which briefly describes the Ninevites' repentance. The author now explains how it came:

> The matter had been heard by the king of Nineveh, so he arose from his throne, removed his kingly robe, covered himself with sackcloth and sat on the ashes. He also summoned and said, "In Nineveh, on behalf of the king and his nobles: Man and beast, the cattle and the sheep, are not to taste anything, not to pasture and not to drink water. They are to cover themselves with sackcloth—man and beast—and call mightily out to God and return each from his evil way and from the (gains of the) violent robbery he has done. Who knows, God may change his mind and repent of his anger, and we will not perish."

In the course of the day that Jonah walked through the city, warning of the coming destruction, the message somehow reached the king of Nineveh himself. "So he arose from his throne, removed his kingly robe, covered himself with sackcloth and sat on the ashes."

The king's first reaction was clear: he accepted personal responsibility for the danger that threatened the city. Somehow, he understood that he could not come before God as one king to another (very much the idea in the ancient Middle East), arrayed in his robes of majesty and authority. He knew that, before God, one must walk softly and humble oneself. We must come as those who have no privileges and no rights, like sinners before our judge.

So the king descended from his throne, removed his kingly robes, clothed himself with sackcloth and sat on ashes as a sign of mourning. Jonah's warning achieved its divinely intended purpose. The inhabitants of the city were moved to repent, beginning with the king and his nobles, all the way down to the simplest of the city's citizens, young or old.

People do not aspire to humility; they prefer honor. Even many Christians are not obviously characterized by their humble attitudes. We try to outdo each other in order to prove that we are better and more successful, hoping that we will gain recognition. We seem not to understand that these ambitions remove us from God's presence, he who "mocks proud mockers but gives grace to the humble" (Prov. 3:34).

We should look to the example of Nineveh's king, who humbled himself and mourned. Why? He mourned for his sin, and so should we.

Our pastors should know how to present the gospel of God's grace in light of his holiness. They should focus on God and his glory rather than on man and his felt needs. Their goal should not be to win friends and influence people, but to follow God and his will. They should not be engaged in church growth strategies but in bringing people into the kingdom of God in humility and repentance.

The gospel is not just the way to happiness but a way to escape the approaching anger. The king of Nineveh did not think of his own happiness—his comfort, dignity or kingly privileges. Instead he thought of the impending punishment and of the sins that were bringing punishment upon him and his people.

When we turn to God, we must do as the king of Nineveh did— approach God with a deep sense of our sinfulness, in shame and sorrow for our sin. It is not enough when people come to Christ, or claim to come to him, simply to escape from a sense of dissatisfaction, to have their problems solved, or to find healing, peace and a purpose for life.

If we come simply because we have been convinced that Jesus is the Messiah, but without any evidence of a recognition of sin in our hearts; if we say we believe but show no humility and no inkling of repentance; if we claim to follow Christ but show no fear of God and no recognition that we need to be cleansed of sin and freed from its grip on our lives; then there is reason to wonder if we have ever been born again by the Spirit.

However, there is no questioning the king of Nineveh's sincerity. He accepted responsibility for his sin, and led all the inhabitants of Nineveh in acknowledging theirs. He issued a royal decree that was announced throughout the city:

> "In Nineveh, on behalf of the king and his nobles: Man and beast, the cattle and the sheep, are not to taste anything, not to pasture and not to drink water. They are to cover themselves with sackcloth—man and beast—and call mightily out to God and return each from his evil way and from the (gains of the) violent robbery he has done. Who knows, God may change his mind and repent of his anger, and we will not perish."

The king instructed all the inhabitants to follow his example and clothe themselves with sackcloth. He further directed them to begin a strict fast: not only were they to avoid eating, but even drinking. They were all to cry out strongly to the Lord. As an expression of their repentance, they were not to feed or water their herds, so that the animals would add their cries of distress to those of the citizens.

However, all of these drastic measures were not enough. Prayer alone would not suffice. The Ninevites all had to do something more, something radical: they had to *return each from his evil way and from the (gains of the) violent robbery he has done.*

In other words, they were required to bring an end to their former way of life and return anything they had taken violently. The Hebrew word for *return* (Yashivu) implies something more than turning (Yashuvu), more than a change of heart. Repentance always involves a change of heart, but that is never where it ends. Real repentance demands action, the kind of action that has moral weight. Repentance means ceasing from sin and undoing whatever harm our sin has done. Obviously, we can't claim to have repented as long as we keep stolen goods in our possession.

Repentance means accepting responsibility for our actions and putting a real effort into making amends. For example, Zaccheus' repentance was obvious when he returned even more than what he had taken unjustly from others. Paul's repentance was clear from his preaching the very gospel he had once opposed. Onesimus repentance was shown when he returned to his owner.

True repentance is never satisfied with mere words. That is why John the Baptist told those who came to him to be baptized that they must bring fruit that is appropriate to repentance (Matt. 3:8). Is there evidence of repentance in your life? Is your life different in any way from the way you lived before? Do you live morally because you have a proper fear of God? Does repentance now characterize your life?

None of us are perfect. None of us have arrived at the point where we never sin or need correction. None of us are free from the need for criticism. Nevertheless it is tempting to reject criticism, to become incensed—openly or secretly—at the very suggestion that we are at fault. We become defensive rather than being receptive to correction.

Let us remind ourselves: who was Jonah? A stranger! And who was the king? The ruler of a great city, famous for its economic and military power. And yet the king responded to this stranger's warnings, and so did his people. Unlike Israel, they had not received God's revelation; they had no divine law to teach them the difference between good and evil. Even their consciences had been eroded by sensuality and idolatry. Still, they repented sincerely, so much so that Christ used them as an example for later generations when he said, *The men of Nineveh will stand up at the judgment with this generation and condemn it; for they repented at the preaching of Jonah* (Matt. 12:41). Will they condemn us too?

How do you respond to criticism? How do you respond when someone remarks negatively about your behavior? How quick are you to examine yourself for any sin in your heart and, if you find any, to turn from it? How open are you to other people's observations about you? Let us see every criticism as an opportunity for self-examination and growth, and let us make the most of every such occasion.

The king signed his decree with the words, "who knows, God may change his mind and repent of his anger, and we will not perish." The captain of the ship in which Jonah tried to escape from the Lord expressed similar sentiments: "Get up, call to your god, it may be that god will think of us and we will not perish" (1:6). We saw there that prayer cannot force God to do anything and that everything depends on his sovereign will. The captain was right when he avoided speaking of God's grace as something to be taken for granted, as if anything we do can guarantee that God will bless us.

This kind of doubt is not a lack of faith but a recognition of God's control over his own grace and of his right to do with us as he sees fit, especially in light of our sin. We should never think that we can force God to give us what we ask for—not even forgiveness. He is the one who rules and we are, at best, his servants. His will is what ought to be carried out, not ours. That is exactly what the king of Nineveh's statement implies. "Who knows, God may change his mind and repent of his anger, and we will not perish." Expressions like "*It may be*" and "*Who knows*" convey the right attitude.

We must preach the gospel with humility, so that those who hear us will learn humility and not think that God is obliged to grant their requests if they just say the right words. We must make clear to our listeners that God owes them nothing, that they have no rights before God. They must not think that if they fast, wear sackcloth and mourn, or do anything else, God will inevitably give them what they want.

Regretfully, the Rabbis and some Christian preachers teach otherwise. The Rabbis, for example, teach that, on the Day of Atonement, Israel can affect the mind of God and determine the course of his decisions. But this is not wisdom. They err greatly. If God forgives sinners, he does so not because of the power of anyone's prayer but because of his loving grace. We can never put God in our debt. We can never bend him to our will. When we come to God, we must come with a humility that recognizes that we depend on him, not he on us: *Who knows, God may change his mind and repent of his anger, and we will not perish.*

God's Response to the People of Nineveh—Verse 10

There is another side to all this: "And the Lord saw from their deeds that they had turned from their evil ways, and the Lord repented of the evil he had said he would do to them, and did not do it." The truth is that God loves to forgive. He does not like to punish. He has no pleasure in the punishment of evil men. Rather, he delights in their repentance and blessing.

The Ninevites' expressions of repentance could not bind God, but his own heart did. He responded to their prayers with a gracious liberality that characterizes our kind, loving, gracious God. As Jonah put it in the next chapter, "I knew you were a merciful and gracious God, patient and full of grace, and that you repent from evil" (4:2).

It is wonderful to be able to turn to such a God. It's easy to seek his forgiveness. Recognition that he is merciful—full of mercy—encourages us to turn to him and away from our sins. Who in his right mind can refuse God's kindness? What kind of person is able to recognize that God is so wonderful, and not love him?

Are we such? Are we quick to forgive? Do we forgive with gladness? Or, God forbid, when people seek our forgiveness, do we insist on humiliating them? Do we hurt them in return and put them in their place as if we have never sinned or harmed others? In this important matter, are we more like God or like his adversary and ours?

"And the Lord saw from their deeds that they had turned from their evil ways, and the Lord repented of the evil he had said he would do to them, and did not do it." The course of action taken by the people of Nineveh had value in God's eyes. Their deeds bore witness to the sincerity of their repentance, "and the Lord repented of the evil he had said he would do to them, and did not do it."

Some think that these last words contradict what we learn elsewhere in the Scriptures, that all of God's actions are both determined and known by him in eternity, and that man cannot change the direction of what God does. That is a mistake. If we read the Scriptures carefully we will see that there is no contradiction. After all, we have seen that the Lord sent Jonah to warn the people of Nineveh because he wanted them to turn from their sins to him. God was the one who determined that the Ninevites would hear the warning, and he did so because he intended them to heed it. He had determined to move the hearts of the inhabitants to repent, and to forgive them in response.

The phrases *the Lord repented of the evil he had said he would do to them, and did not do it* and *repent from evil* (4:2) do not indicate any kind of change in God. They speak of the intended results of the change that took place in the hearts of the people of Nineveh. God created this change by sending Jonah to address the city. Salvation is wholly an act of God. Faith and repentance are also his gifts, the product of the saving work of the Holy Spirit.

When referring to God, the term *repent* is an anthropomorphism, a description of God as if he had human characteristics. There is no better way to describe what happened in spite of the shortcoming involved in using human terms to describe divine action. As C. S. Lewis once put it, "God is at least a person" and that is the most we are able to say about him. Human terms are the highest available to us. So, when speaking of God, the term *repent* does not refer to a change in God's plans or intentions. It indicates God's blessing on the people of Nineveh in response to their repentance, which in turn came in response to Jonah's preaching—which God had also blessed.

There is tremendous encouragement for us in these truths. We learn that God hears prayer and that he responds. God forgives sinners if they repent and turn to him. God wants people to turn from their evil ways and return from the violence which is in their hands; he wants them to mend their lifestyles according to his word. When they do so, he treats them with kindness and generosity. So let's not embrace and protect our sins. Let's leave them behind, and find in God the forgiveness that we so much need.

Sisters and brothers, if you are struggling at this time with some sin—turn from it. If you hesitate to ask for forgiveness and to correct something you have done—stop hesitating. Grace is calling. It invites you: come to God and find peace.

Prayer

O God,
sin lives in us, grips us, enslaves us,
keeps us from doing good.
We hate it and want to be rid of it.
Give us strength.
In spite of our sin, give us strength,
conquer our sin for us and drive us away from it,
and forgive us in the name of your Son, our great Savior,
Jesus, the Messiah, Amen.

Questions for Discussion

1. What is true repentance? How is it shown? Have you truly repented? When and how?

2. What essentials of saving faith are described in this chapter?

3. Is God obliged to forgive those who pray to him? On what grounds does he forgive?

4. Summarize what else you have learned about God's forgiveness and how you should forgive.

5. Does God change his mind?

7

Jonah Prophesies in Nineveh

3:10–4:11

∗

And God saw their deeds, that they had returned from their evil way, and God repented of the evil he had determined to do to them, and did not do it.

This was to Jonah a very great evil, and he was angry. And he prayed to the Lord and said, "Please Lord, was this not what I thought when I was still on my land?! That is why I at first tried to escape to Tarshish, because, I knew you were a merciful and gracious God, patient and full of grace, and that you repent from evil! Now, Lord, please take my life from me, because my death is to be preferred to my life."

And the Lord said, "Are you very angry?!"

And Jonah went out of the city and sat east of the city and built himself there a booth, and sat under it in the shade until he would see what will happen to the city.

And God appointed a gourd, which grew above Jonah to be a shade over his head, to save him from his evil. And Jonah was very happy over the gourd.

And God appointed a worm at dusk the next day, which gnawed the gourd and it shriveled. When the sun rose, God appointed a quiet eastern wind, and the sun smote on Jonah's head and he became faint, and wished to die, saying, "My death is to be preferred to my life."

And God said to Jonah, "Are you right to be angry over the gourd?" So he responded—I am right to be angry—to the point of death!" Then the Lord said, "You had pity on the gourd, for which you did not labor and did not cultivate, that came up in a night and was lost in a night—and I should not have pity on Nineveh, that great city in which there are more than 120,000 humans who do not know between their right and their left, and many animals?!"

Chapter 4 is the heart of the book of Jonah because it reveals the punch line. Chapters 1–3 introduce the characters and situations, give us the background, and build to this point. Here we find the book's central lesson and learn what God taught Jonah, from which we can draw important conclusions for ourselves.

God's Response to the Ninevites' Actions—Verse 10

"And God saw their deeds, that they had returned from their evil way, and God repented of the evil he had determined to do to them, and did not do it." From the last words of this verse—*and did not do it* to them—we understand that forty days had passed from the day Jonah began declaring Nineveh's coming destruction. During those forty days, Nineveh's people, led by the king and his nobles, fasted, wore sackcloth, sat on ashes, withheld food and water from their animals, and cried out to the Lord. Day after day they called on him. Day after day they went through their routines fearing the punishment that was about to fall on them. Their repentance was not partial or superficial. It lasted forty long days.

We must beware of expecting instant results when we declare the gospel. People who ask God to forgive their sins expect an immediate response. Preachers must not assume the role of the Holy Spirit by assuring those who merely say the sinner's prayer that they have been forgiven. They must not teach that all that is necessary for salvation is to believe in the message. Belief alone does not change the heart—the core of our being. Teaching that it does empties the gospel of its content and robs it of its power. If there is no spiritual shame before God and no sorrow over sin, then the resulting "conversion" is the product of human manipulation rather than the work of the Spirit of God. In consequence, such supposed new births are artificial. They are still-born and worldly rather than being true birth from above, by the Spirit.

All too often the biblical idea of faith has been exchanged for simple intellectual or emotional assent. In contrast, the biblical perspective teaches that assurance of salvation is the work of the Holy Spirit, and that true salvation results in people really turning from the depths of their hearts to God in humble repentance. God himself is active in conversions like these. He sends his Holy Spirit and people are born again by the Spirit's power.

Sometimes we must pray for days, weeks and months, asking God to forgive our sins and to grant us a part in the salvation Jesus has purchased with his blood. This involves examining our hearts and discovering more and more of our sin. As we do this, we understand God's greatness more and more and recognize our unworthiness before him. This, then, brings us to a sense of our need for forgiveness and for a transformed life. When, at last, the Holy Spirit begins to comfort us and to give us a sense of forgiveness in our hearts, we are changed significantly. From that time on our lives bear the stamp of the gospel. Old things have passed, and everything has become new. We begin to focus on our struggle against sin, on holiness, and on glorifying God.

We must beware of a short and easy gospel. To the extent that it is short and easy, it is also superficial. People hear the gospel, pray and—just like that—they're saved! There is no pleading, no humility, no fear and no honor to God. It's all about the individual and his or her happiness.

The results of this type of "gospel" are telling. As long as anyone claims salvation but remains in their sins, there is reason to doubt whether the Holy Spirit has ever worked in their lives. In these cases, any change in their lives seems superficial. It does not reach down into the depths of their souls, their view of themselves in the sight of God and their sense of duty to him. They have never cried out, like the prophet, *I am ruined! I am a man of unclean lips, and I live among a people of unclean lips, and my eyes have seen the King, the LORD Almighty* (Isa. 6:5). They never acknowledge their sin in such a way that they said, *Go away from me, Lord; I am a sinful man!* (Luke 5:8). They take their supposed salvation for granted.

That is not how the Ninevites viewed things. They cried out to God for forty days. "And God saw their deeds, that they had turned from their evil way, and God repented of the evil he had determined to do to them, and did not do it."

Does what we do before God indicate the sincerity of our repentance? God is able to see our most hidden thoughts. He looks at what we do. Does he see more than mere religious words, self-pity and the desire for happiness?

Jonah Responds to the Grace of God—Verses 1–3

We would expect that a servant of God who is sent to warn people that God is about to punish them for their sins would be delighted to see those people glorifying God and accepting his lordship over them, repenting of their sin and pleading with God for mercy and forgiveness. That was not Jonah's response.

We would expect that a servant of the Lord would rejoice when the word of God takes effect and those who hear it respond in faith. That was not Jonah's response.

We would expect that whoever serves the Lord would seek to model his heart after the Lord's and to love what the Lord loves. That was not Jonah's response.

Instead, Nineveh's repentance *was to Jonah a very great evil, and he was angry.* The prophet was furious. He was saddened by the grace shown to Nineveh. He dared to see something undesirable, something inappropriate in what God had done.

Scripture does not tell us why Jonah saw things this way. Was he jealous for Israel and thought that they were the only ones who should receive God's grace? Did he care so much for Israel that he dreaded the threat Nineveh might pose if its people were not destroyed? We don't know, and there is no point in trying to guess. It is not important, because Scripture does not clearly explain Jonah's reaction. Rather, what is important is that Jonah dared think that way at all.

Is there anything that God does that you consider inappropriate? When God blesses those who oppose you, are you jealous? Does the thought cross your mind that things should be different? When God bring trials and difficulties into your life, do you think that you deserve an easier path, a bit more comfort and a bit more ease? When someone else receives praise and attention, are you jealous?

"This was to Jonah a very great evil, and he was angry. And he prayed to the Lord and said, 'Please Lord, was this not what I thought when I was still on my land?! That is why I at first tried to escape to Tarshish, because, I knew you were a merciful and gracious God, patient and full of grace, and that you repent from evil!'"

Jonah flings in God's face what should have moved the prophet to worship. He complains about what should have brought joy and criticizes God for the very reason for which he should have praised him. That is why he tried to escape God at the beginning of our narrative: he knew that God was merciful. He understood that the Lord had sent him to Nineveh to save its inhabitants from the punishment they deserved for their sins—and that is exactly what he did not want to happen! What God considered good was, in Jonah's eyes, *a very great evil*.

Where did such arrogant brashness come from, and how could it have hidden in the heart of a servant of the Lord? It will be difficult for us to answer the second question, but we know the answer to the first: that arrogance is hidden in every person's heart. We all think that we are entitled to judge God's actions. By what right does God decide to forgive one and to condemn another for his sin? After all, there were many sinful cities in Jonah's day, but Jonah was only sent to Nineveh. Somehow, we think it unjust for God to prefer one individual or nation over another.

We really tend to think that God must for some reason meet our moral standards, and that when he does not act as we think fit, we have the right to be angry. Sin is in all of us; that sin drives us to a terrible pride.

Isaiah responded to such arrogance when he said, "Woe to him who quarrels with his Maker, to him who is but a potsherd among the potsherds on the ground. Does the clay say to the potter, 'What are you making?' Does your work say, 'He has no hands'? Woe to him who says to his father, 'What have you begotten?' or to his mother, 'What have you brought to birth?'" (Isa. 45:9–10). Paul agrees when he asks, "Who are you, O man, to talk back to God? Shall what is formed say to him who formed it, 'Why did you make me like this?'" (Rom. 9:20)?

We are certainly invited by the Bible to inquire after the logic of God's actions. But we may do this only as an expression of humble faith, never out of an arrogance that dares to challenge and demand an answer. Christians are people who ask questions, who wonder after the nature of things and events. But they never think they have the right to expect God to act according to their logic or prove to them the wisdom and justice of his deeds. God owes and will give account to no one!

We asked, "How could such arrogant brashness find a place in the heart of a servant of God?" The truth is that we all are full of contradictions. We are saved from sin and yet keep falling back to sin. We love God but not with all our hearts. We want the good of the church but often find it hard to sacrifice for that good. We want something to happen but do not do what is necessary to make it happen.

Those who serve the Lord are subject to greater temptations. Satan focuses on them because he understands that if he can cause one of them to stumble, many others will be affected. That is why we need to pray continually for those who serve us, while watching over them, visiting them, loving them, and encouraging them to constant growth in their devotion, self examination, sacrifice and self denial.

> This was to Jonah a very great evil, and he was angry. And he prayed to the Lord and said, "Please Lord, was this not what I thought when I was still on my land?! That is why I at first tried to escape to Tarshish, because, I knew you were a merciful and gracious God, patient and full of grace, and that you repent from evil! Now, Lord, please take my life from me, because my death is to be preferred to my life."

God's plan disturbed Jonah so greatly that he preferred death to living with reality. Up to this point he knew God was kind and merciful, but in his heart of hearts he hoped that, somehow, it might be otherwise. But his hope was disappointed and he revolted against this so radically, so deeply, that he preferred to die than submit to it. He did not want to live with such a God in control of things.

Nothing exalts God more than his grace, and nothing humbles us more, robs us of any grounds for boasting and exposes our utter failure more than that same grace—because it is given apart from any of our achievements or human worth.

Similarly, nothing is more painful than such a radical revolution in the way we see things. If we are used to thinking in terms of earning favor, we will find it difficult to accept any other terms. If we are used to thinking that everything depends on us, we will find it difficult to understand that everything depends on God.

God Responds to Jonah—Verse 4

God did not leave Jonah in that terrible state of rebellion. He once again showed Jonah the same grace he had shown him when the prophet had tried to escape, the same grace he had shown to Nineveh. He determined to conquer Jonah's heart and change his mind. Just as there was no limit to what the Lord was willing to do to cause the prophet to obey him, so he acted again to teach Jonah his ways.

> And the Lord said, "Are you very angry?!"
>
> And Jonah went out of the city and sat east of the city and built himself there a booth, and sat under it in the shade until he would see what will happen to the city.
>
> And God appointed a gourd, which grew above Jonah to be a shade over his head, to save him from his evil. And Jonah was very happy over the gourd.
>
> And God appointed a worm at dusk the next day, which gnawed the gourd and it shriveled. When the sun rose, God appointed a quiet eastern wind, and the sun smote on Jonah's head and he became faint, and wished to die, saying, "My death is to be preferred to my life."
>
> And God said to Jonah, "Are you right to be angry over the gourd?" So he responded—"I am right to be angry—to the point of death!" Then the Lord said, "You had pity on the gourd, from which you did not labor and did not cultivate, that came up in a night and was lost in a night—and I should not have pity on Nineveh, that great city in which there are more than 120,000 humans who do not know between their right and their left, and many animals?!"

The Lord began with a question geared to motivate Jonah to examine himself: *"Are you very angry?!"* This question has a double meaning. First, "Are you thoroughly angry?" Second, "Are you right to be angry?" The Hebrew allows for both readings. They invite the prophet to examine his anger so that he will see the error of his response.

But Jonah was very much like us, and he was not interested in self-examination. He was too busy criticizing God's actions to investigate his own. This reminds us that while self-examination is one of the most necessary of the Christian duties, it is also one of the most difficult.

With the question, "Are you very angry?" ringing in his ears, he "went out of the city and sat east of the city and built himself there a booth, and sat under it in the shade." Impolitely, brashly, he turned his back to God and walked away. The conversation was too uncomfortable, too threatening.

In addition, Jonah still entertained a hope that God would see things his way and alter his plan so that Nineveh would be punished. He broke off conversation, left the city, established himself to its east, built a booth and sat to wait until he would see what would happen to the city.

Mercifully, God had not completed his work with the prophet. He, the Master of All, continued to take action: "And God appointed a gourd, which grew above Jonah to be a shade over his head, to save him from his evil. And Jonah was very happy over the gourd."

God is stubborn in his love and will not leave us in our sins. He had appointed the fish at the right time and place, and now he appointed a gourd that grew beside Jonah's booth, providing better shade from the scorching desert heat.

The author again employs a term that can be read in more than one way when he says that the gourd was meant *to save him from his evil*. Jonah's language, we have said, is rich and highly suggestive. Its very ambivalence is meant to guide us into thinking about these events and learning appropriate lessons from them.

Our rendering has focused on what I believe to be the primary meaning of the text, but it can also be taken to read, as do many of the translations, "to give shade for his head to ease his discomfort" (NIV). As the story unfolds we discover that the gourd served God to teach the prophet a lesson, and that the lesson had to do with less than worthy attitudes in Jonah's heart.

It's good to know that God does not give up, that he will not allow the evil of our hearts to remain there. Sometimes a deep plowing is needed, but God is willing to carry out this painful process and save us from evil.

Jonah enjoyed the shade provided by the gourd, and "was very happy over the gourd." But that joy was intended by God to serve a higher purpose than the prophet's comfort, which is why God also cut it short: "And God appointed a worm at dusk the next day, which gnawed the gourd and it shriveled. When the sun rose, God appointed a quiet eastern wind, and the sun smote on Jonah's head."

God blessed Jonah with the gourd, and he took the gourd from him. Both were acts of God. That is how it is in our lives. Sometimes God makes it easier for us, and sometimes he makes it harder, but he always works for a higher goal than our comfort or pleasure. We tend to forget this and to examine things from the perspective of immediate satisfaction, however temporary. We delight in a gourd that shades us from the sun, and when it dies we respond like Jonah: He *wished to die, saying, "My death is to be preferred to my life."*

I'm sure you will agree with me that both Jonah's joy and his disappointment were exaggerated. He was tossed between an unreasonably exultant joy and an illogically deep sadness. He *wished to die, saying, "My death is to be preferred to my life,"* all over a gourd! Do we never exaggerate in our responses? Do we tend to value the temporary while neglecting the eternal? Do the momentary pleasures or pains we experience really count in light of eternity? Sisters and brothers, look at life in broad terms, in light of eternity, and not in light of what is here today and gone tomorrow.

God again invites Jonah to examine himself: *And God said to Jonah, "Are you right to be angry over the gourd?"* Are you thoroughly angry over the withering of the gourd? Is it right for you to be angry? Jonah's response is one of terrible arrogance: *I am right to be angry—to the point of death!* I am very angry, and I am right to be angry like this, to the point that I prefer to die! Remember, Jonah is talking to God. This little germ of a creature is shaking his fist at his eternal Maker, and and yet God does not destroy him in a moment but instead bears with him in infinite patience. What a glorious God Jonah had.

The Lord responds to Jonah's terse reply in grace, wooing him away from his terrible arrogance and from his narrow view of things: "You had pity on the gourd, for which you did not labor and did not cultivate, that came up in a night and was lost in a night—and I should not have pity on Nineveh, that great city in which there are more than 120,000 humans who do not know between their right and their left, and many animals?!" Or perhaps, "You showed sorrow over the loss of a miserable gourd—don't you think I should have some concern over a city as big as Nineveh, in which over 120,000 of its inhabitants can't tell between good and evil?" It is possible the number 120,000 refers to the number of children in the city. It is also possible that the number refers to the total population, but we don't really know for certain. What we do know is the more important fact that Jonah wanted the city and its inhabitants, young or old, man and beast, destroyed. He did not show even a shred of mercy or kindness. Yet God was kind toward Jonah. Such is the nature of our God. Such are the riches of his grace.

Jonah was delighted over the gourd because it was useful to him. His joy was purely selfish. His anger over the loss of the gourd was likewise selfish, and yet the prophet dared to think he was right. That is the sum of the prophet's sin. Self-centered, self-loving, self-serving in spite of his calling and in spite of the liberality of the kindness shown toward him, Jonah could not understand why God would rejoice over the Ninevites' repentance. Can we?

So often we are like Jonah. We are commanded, *freely you have received, freely give. Receive one another as Christ has received us to the glory of God. As I have loved you, so should you love one another.* We have been forgiven so very much, yet seem to be tight-fisted and mean when it comes to forgiving others.

Everything exists for the glory of God and the execution of his will, just as the gourd served to provide the prophet with shade. Jonah was pleased with the comfort he derived from the gourd, and God expects to be glorified in mankind, by their good deeds and their loving fear of him. Did Jonah have a right God does not have? *You had pity on the gourd,* God says—*and I should not have pity on Nineveh?*

God wanted the inhabitants of Nineveh to be saved, to glorify him by their repentance, just as Jonah wanted the gourd to continue to provide him with shade. Which of the two has more right to what he wants? For whom does the world, with all its gourds and the inhabitants of all its cities, exist? Like Jonah, we are often embittered in the face of difficulty, as if we deserve happiness and the world exists just to make us happy. Then we become angry when kindness is shown to someone who has hurt us, or someone we dislike is blessed. Such an attitude puts us where only God should be: at the center of the universe. What terrible pride!

We need to learn from the book of Jonah: Even though God entered into covenant with Israel alone, he is the God of all nations and is to be glorified in them all. Likewise, God is not only the Lord of the Reformed, or the Charismatic; of the Baptists or the Presbyterians; of Jews or of Gentiles. He is Lord over all and loves to show his kindness to all. Simply because the inhabitants of Nineveh belonged to the human race, their salvation was important to God.

This is the central message of the book of Jonah. Jonah did not create the gourd, but the God of Israel created the inhabitants of Nineveh and all who live in this world. They all belong to him and they all owe him a debt of honor, love and obedience. He will be glorified in them all, and he desires the salvation of them all. We must never try to limit the goodness of God to ourselves, to those who agree with us or to those who for any reason are dear to us.

There is an especially important lesson for the people of Israel, who allow themselves to think that God loves none but the Jewish people. The Jewish believers in the apostolic church were inclined to such a mistaken notion. So they tried to convince Gentile believers to become Jewish. That was a mistake we ought not to repeat. "God does not show favouritism but accepts men from every nation who fear him and do what is right" (Acts 10:34–35).

✳

The unknown author did not continue with the story of Jonah. He did not describe to us how Jonah responded to the divine challenge that the book's final question poses. The Holy Spirit guided him to end the narrative here, so that we too would have to face the piercing question:

Do we care for others, or are we like Jonah? Do we long for the salvation of others, or are we busy with our own concerns? Are we willing to welcome others into the circle of those we love and serve, or do we prefer to love those who love us and seek the company of the pleasant and easy-going? Do we love others because of what we get from them, or do we love them because our hearts are motivated by a loving fear of the God who created all mankind, and we must therefore love all? Are we like Jonah or what God calls us to be?

A Jewish tradition insists that, in response to the question, Jonah fell on his face and acknowledged God's right to rule in his world by grace, as it is said: "The Lord our God is merciful and forgiving, even though we have rebelled against him" (Dan. 9:9). We do not know if Jonah responded in this way, but it is certainly the right way to respond. We should relate to others with the same grace with which God relates to us.

Summary

1. We should be wary of selfishness. It is never right to evaluate people by what they can do for us. Everyone and

everything exist for the glory of God, and that is why all people have value.

2. God invites us to ask, wonder and investigate. But he does not invite us to rebel and doubt his higher wisdom.

3. God deals with us in kindness and endless patience in spite of our sins. He is a God of amazing goodness. When we sin he will bear with us by his goodness and correct what is wrong in us.

4. God is the Lord of all nations and of all people. He cares for each one and from them all he chooses those who will be saved. We must learn to love as God loves, and to incorporate all mankind within our loving embrace. This message is an important stage in the preparation of Israel for the coming of the gospel, through which God is creating one new people in Christ, made up of Jews and of Gentiles, males and females, slaves and freeman. There is to be no difference between them.

Prayer

O God of all nations and of every human being,
who created all things for your own glory.
shape our heart so that it will be more like your own.
Teach us to love what you love
and not to put ourselves in the center of our lives.
That place is reserved for you.
Teach us to place you at the center,
and when we sin against you—
for there is not a single person who never sins—
forgive us for Jesus your Son's sake, Amen

Questions for Discussion

1. What new lessons have you learned about the nature of true faith?

2. What new lessons have you learned about the way the gospel should be preached?

3. What was wrong with the prophet's response to God's grace toward the Ninevites? Do you ever respond similarly?

4. Summarize God's attitude to Jonah in response to the prophet's anger. What does this teach you about God?

5. Why did God address Jonah with questions and what should we learn from that?

Final Summary Questions for Discussion

Summarize the lessons of the book of Jonah on the following topics:

1. God, his character and his dealings with man
2. God and his control of all
3. Man and his relationship with God
4. Law and covenant
5. Grace
6. Faith
7. Repentance
8. Forgiveness
9. Good will toward others
10. The Word of God
11. Prayer